TABLE OF CONTENTS

Page

TABLES

CHAPTER 1

INTRODUCTION

Following his election in February 2010, Ukraine's President Viktor Yanukovych

made European Union integration a priority and within a week of his inauguration, he

traveled to Brussels for his first official foreign visit. "For Ukraine, European integration

is the key priority of its foreign policy," Yanukovych told European Commission

President José Manuel Barroso. In addition, Yanukovych referred to European integration

as "a strategy for systemic social and economic reforms."[1] Indeed, starting as early as the

1990s, under Leonid Kuchma's presidency, Ukraine has regularly expressed its willing-

ness to participate in European integration. On June 14, 1994, the European Union and

Ukraine started a political dialogue when the two signed a Partnership and Cooperation

Agreement that despite nearly four years of delay in ratification by the member states,

entered into force on March 1, 1998.[2] The Partnership and Cooperation Agreement

---

[1]UkrainianJournal.com, "Yanukovych: EU relations a 'key priority,'" March 1, 2010, http://www.ukrainianjournal.com (accessed March 15, 2012).

[2]The Partnership and Cooperation Agreement (PCA) between the European Communities and their Member States and Ukraine provided a comprehensive and ambitious framework for cooperation between the European Union and Ukraine. It expired in March 2008. At a Paris Summit in September 2008, the European Union and Ukraine agreed to begin negotiations on a European Union-Ukraine Association Agreement, which is to be the successor agreement to the PCA. http://ec.europa.eu/ world/agreements/for the full text of the PCA (accessed March 15, 2012). For an outline of the political and legal foundations of the PCA, as well as the institutional framework, see, European Union External Action Service, "EU-Ukraine Relations," http://www.eeas. europa.eu/ukraine/pdf/political_and_legal_foundations.pdf (accessed March 15, 2012).

served later as a basis for a Joint European Union-Ukraine Action Plan endorsed by the European Council on February 21, 2005.[3]

Ukraine's relationship vis-à-vis the European Union has become increasingly relevant in recent years, particularly after the 2004 Orange Revolution.[4] The European Union considers Ukraine to be a priority partner within the European Neighbourhood Policy and Ukraine is one of six post-Soviet states invited to cooperate with the European Union within the multilateral framework of the Eastern Partnership Project.[5] Ukraine deputy premier Hryhoriy Nemyria expressed enthusiasm about the project stating that it is the way to modernize Ukraine since the Eastern Partnership relies upon instruments

---

[3]A March 2008 Joint Evaluation Report describes the Action Plan as "a day-to-day tool for guiding and monitoring European Union-Ukraine cooperation and as an instrument to move forward the reform process in Ukraine." See, European Commission, European Neighbourhood Policy, http://ec.europa.eu/world/enp/partners/enp_ukraine_ en.htm (accessed March 15, 2012).

[4]The Orange Revolution was a series of protests and political events that took place in Kyiv from November 2004 to January 2005, in the immediate aftermath of a disputed run-off vote of the 2004 Ukrainian presidential election. See, Paul D'Anieri, ed., *Orange Revolution and Aftermath: Mobilization, Apathy, and the State in Ukraine* (Baltimore: Johns Hopkins University Press, 2010).

[5]The European Union's Eastern Partnership includes the post-Soviet states of Belarus, Ukraine, Moldova, Azerbaijan, Armenia and Georgia. Poland, with the assistance of Sweden, proposed this project at the European Union's General Affairs and External Relations Council in Brussels on May 26, 2008. Eastern Partnership was inaugurated on May 7, 2009. It aims to improve political and economic trade relations of the six strategically important partner countries, and strives to promote democracy, human rights and the rule of law. See, Eastern Partnership, European External Action Service, http://eeas.europa.eu/ eastern/index_en.htm (accessed March 15, 2012). See also, Elena Korosteleva, ed., *Eastern Partnership: A New Opportunity for the Neighbours?* (London: Routledge, 2011).

similar to those for European Union candidates.[6] In February 2008, the European Union

and Ukraine started negotiations aimed at establishing a free trade area offering a legal

framework for closer economic cooperation and enhanced political dialogue.[7] A few

months later, the European Union and Ukraine agreed that the free trade area should be

part of an Association Agreement designed to be the successor to the Partnership and

Cooperation Agreement.[8]

Plans for the European Commission and Ukraine entering into a free trade area

and signing an Association Agreement stalled in late 2011, however, as a result of the

European Union's criticism of what it perceives as the politically motivated trial of

---

[6]Valentina Pop, "EU Expanding Its 'Sphere of Influence,' Russia Says," EUObserver.com, March 21, 2009, http://euobserver.com/24/27827 (accessed March 15, 2012).

[7]A free trade area is a trade bloc whose member countries have signed a free trade agreement, which eliminates tariffs, import quotas, and preferences on most, if not all, goods and services traded between them. If people are also free to move between the countries, in addition to a free trade agreement, it would also be considered an Open Border. It can be considered the second stage of economic integration. Countries choose this kind of economic integration if their economic structures are complementary. If their economic structures are competitive, they are more likely to form a customs union.

[8]Unian, "New Enhanced Agreement Between Ukraine and EU Called 'Agreement on Association'," July 22, 2008, http://www.unian.net/eng/news/263031-new-enhanced-agreement-between-ukraine-and-eu-called-agreement-on-association (accessed March 15, 2012). An Association Agreement is a treaty between the European Union and a non-member state that creates a framework for cooperation and the development of political, trade, social, cultural and security links. The legal basis for concluding an Association Agreement is provided by Art. 217 Treaty on the Functioning of the European Union (former Art. 310 Treaty establishing the European Community). See, *4th Joint Progress Report on Negotiations on the EU-Ukraine Association Agreement*, Brussels/Kyiv, November 8, 2010, http://eeas.europa.eu/ukraine/docs/joint_progress_ report4_ association_en.pdf (accessed March 15, 2012).

former Ukrainian Prime Minister Yulia Tymoshenko.[9] On October 11, 2011, a Ukrainian

court sentenced Tymoshenko to seven years in prison after she was found guilty of abuse

of office after brokering a 2009 gas deal with Russia.[10] The trial and conviction of

Tymoshenko have raised questions concerning Yanukovich's leadership, the

independence of Ukraine's judiciary, and Ukraine's commitment to the values of

mainstream Europe.[11] The European Union views Tymoshenko's trial and conviction as

"justice being applied selectively under political motivation."[12] Brussels has stated that

by imprisoning Ukraine's most important opposition activist, "Kyiv is torpedoing its own

aspirations to Europe."[13] According to Amanda Paul of the European Policy Centre, "the

---

[9]Unian, "Yanukovych: Ukraine and EU have agreed on Association Agreement full text," December 20, 2011, http://www.unian.net/eng/news/475511-yanukovych-ukraine-and-eu-have-agreed-on-association-agreement-full-text.html (accessed March 15, 2012). Tymoshenko served as prime minister under President Victor Yushchenko from January 24, 2005 until September 8, 2005. She was appointed a second time following Yushchenko's 2007 election win, serving from December 18, 2007 until March 4, 2010. A candidate in the Ukrainian presidential elections of 2010, she lost to Yanukovych.

[10]Euronews, "EU feels let down by Ukraine over Tymoshenko," October 11, 2011, http://www.euronews. net/2011/10/11/eu-feels-let-down-by-ukraine-over-tymoshenko/ (accessed March 15, 2012).

[11]See, BBC News Europe, "Q&A: Ukraine's Yulia Tymoshenko on trial," October 11, 2011, http://www.bbc.co.uk/news/world-europe-14459446 (accessed March 15, 2012). Citing "a number of recent domestic developments in Ukraine [which] have led to a difficult atmosphere between the European Union and Ukraine," President van Rompuy stated that the long-awaited deal outlining political and economic cooperation between Kyiv and Brussels has been finalized, but its signing hinges on Tymoshenko's fate. See, Maria Danilova, "EU-Ukraine pact finalized, signing stalled," December 19, 2011, http://www. theolympian.com/2011/12/19/v-print/1918764/ukraine-eu-summit-clouded-by-tymoshenkos.html (accessed March 15, 2012).

[12]Euronews, "EU feels let down by Ukraine over Tymoshenko."

[13]Nicu Popescu, "EU?–No Thanks!" Eastern Partnership Community, December 9, 2011, http://www.easternpartnership.org/community/debate/eu-no-thanks (accessed

European Union finds itself in quite a difficult situation now. Clearly it wants to remain engaged with Ukraine because Ukraine is an important country and these agreements can have a significant impact on changing things in Ukraine. But at the same time it is obvious from the signals that they cannot allow what happened . . . to go by unnoticed or without affecting the relationship."[14] In addition to forming the latest chapter in Ukraine's relationship with the European Union, Tymoshenko's trial and conviction offer a poignant irony to Ukraine's efforts at seeking increased European integration. During a 2003 interview, Tymoshenko, then a member of Ukraine's Parliament, paraphrased Konstantin Stanislavsky, Russian theater director, actor, and theorist, and declared that "Ukrainians should love not ourselves in Europe but Europe in ourselves. The more life in Ukraine approaches the European level (by its quality, prosperity, democracy, humaneness), the more evident is the country's orientation to the West. And, if Europeans help us on this way, we will appreciate their interest."[15] Could Tymoshenko have envisioned eight years after her remarks embracing European integration, that her own trial and conviction would be the cause behind the deterioration of Ukraine-European Union relations?

This thesis researches the complex relationship between the European Union and Ukraine. It examines the progress of Ukraine's integration with the European Union in

---

March 15, 2012). Popescu concludes: "Ukraine, ostentatiously and with theatrical panache, has charged Tymoshenko with further wrongdoings."

[14]Euronews, "EU feels let down by Ukraine over Tymoshenko."

[15]Center for Peace, Conversion and Foreign Policy of Ukraine, *European Integration of Ukraine as Viewed by Top Ukrainian Politicians, Businessmen and Society Leaders* (Warsaw: Center for Peace, Conversion and Foreign Policy of Ukraine, 2003), 30.

the years following the 2004 Orange Revolution.[16] In the Association Agenda adopted by the European Union-Ukraine Cooperation Council on November 23, 2009, the European Union cited the Orange Revolution as demonstrating "Ukraine's determination to deepen the process of domestic democratic reform."[17] In addition, the May 1, 2004 Eastern enlargement of the European Union established a direct border with Ukraine.[18] Recognizing their "increasingly dynamic relationship," the Association Agenda cited these developments as creating an "opportunity for the European Union and Ukraine to move beyond cooperation towards gradual integration and deepening political association."[19] Moreover, if Ukraine succeeds in integrating into the European Union, it could lead to a change in the geopolitical dynamics of Eastern Europe and the South Caucasus resulting in a westward pull on other states in the region, especially Georgia and Moldova. Nonetheless, despite publicly advocating increased integration with the European Union, Ukraine's political leadership is often criticized for not embracing a more spirited policy of Europeanization. This research explores the question of whether Ukraine is undergoing the process of Europeanization, that is, whether it is pursuing

---

[16]The Orange Revolution was a series of protests and political events that took place in Kyiv from November 2004 to January 2005, in the immediate aftermath of a disputed run-off vote of the 2004 Ukrainian presidential election. See, D'Anieri, ed., *Orange Revolution and Aftermath.*

[17]European Commission, European Union-Ukraine Association Agenda to prepare and facilitate the implementation of the Association Agreement, 1, http://www. eeas.europa.eu/ukraine/docs/2010_eu_ukraine_association_agenda_en.pdf (accessed March 15, 2012).

[18]Ukraine borders the member states of Hungary, Poland, Romania and Slovakia.

[19]Ibid.

institutional reforms and adopting European Union law in an effort to further integrate

with Europe that may lead eventually to Ukraine's membership in the European Union.

Defining European Integration and Europeanization

This research addresses European integration and the process of Europeanization

in post-2004 Ukraine. Before introducing the primary and secondary questions of this

research, it may prove helpful to identify and define these terms which though related are

not synonymous. Writing about Europe in the mid-1950s, Ernst B. Haas, German-

American political scientist and international relations theorist, broadly defined

integration as the process "whereby political actors in several, distinct national settings

are persuaded to shift their loyalties, expectations and political activities toward a new

centre, whose institutions possess or demand jurisdiction over the pre-existing national

states."[20] Haas' definition of integration encompasses both a social and political process

of European integration envisioned by the "new centre" established by the European

Economic Community. Recently, political scientists Thomas Dietz and Antje Wiener

have defined European integration as "the process of intensifying political cooperation in

Europe and the development of common political institutions" including the "changing

constructions of identities of social actors in the context of this process."[21] Within the

context of the European Union, integration refers to establishing closer links between the

European Union and its member states and citizens through shared aims, common laws

---

[20]Ernst B. Haas, *The Uniting of Europe: Political, Social, and Economic Forces 1950-57* (Stanford, CA: Stanford University Press, 1958), 16.

[21]Thomas Diez and Antje Wiener, "Introducing the Mosaic of Integration Theory," in *European Integration Theory*, ed. Antje Wiener and Thomas Diez, 2d. ed. (Oxford: Oxford University Press, 2009), 4.

and institutions. It would be incorrect, however, to limit one's definition of European integration solely to that of the European Union and its member states. Indeed, "Europe" is sometimes used in a geopolitically limiting way to refer only to the European Union. A more comprehensive definition of European integration encompasses political, economic, legal, social and cultural integration of states located wholly or partially in Europe.

Related to the study of European integration is the process of Europeanization. Typically, Europeanization refers to "the process of institutional transformation under-way in countries that are members of, or applicants to, the European Union."[22] It is "a process of transformation within a state introduced by the external environment of the European Union on domestic politics."[23] Political scientist Claudio Radaelli defines Europeanization as the incorporation of "formal and informal rules, procedures, policy paradigms, styles, 'ways of doing things', and shared beliefs and norms, which are first defined and consolidated in the making of European Union public policy and politics . . . in the logic of domestic discourse, identities, political structures, and public policies."[24] It is common to define the process of European integration "along the lines of internal and

---

[22]Melinda Kovács and Olena Leipnik, "The Borders of Orientalism: 'Europeanization' in Hungary and Ukraine," *Debatte* 16, no. 2 (August 2008): 151-169, 151-152.

[23]Katarzyna Kuszewska, "The Challenges of Europeanization: On the Example of Poland-the New Member State of the EU," *E-Magazine*, http://www.cailaw.org/academy/magazine/Europeanization-article.pdf (accessed March 18, 2012).

[24]Claudio Radaelli, "The Europeanization of Public Policy," in *The Politics of Europeanization*, ed. Kevin Featherstone and Claudio Radelli (Oxford: Oxford University Press, 2003), 30.

external Europeanization."[25] Internal Europeanization refers to the process in which the national interests of a member state of the European Union become European interests and involves the adoption of a common set of norms, values and institutions, the implementation of common rules, and "continuous interaction, regular consultation and communication" among the member states.[26] External Europeanization, on the other hand, involves the projection of European Union norms and values and system of governance to those countries outside the European Union.[27] The external aspect of Europeanization is the focus of this research which examines the bilateral relations between Ukraine and the European Union.

Research Question

Is Ukraine undergoing the process of Europeanization? Specifically, is Ukraine adopting the necessary domestic reforms and legislative changes within its economic and energy sectors and its judiciary consistent with the rules, procedures and values of the European Union? Secondary questions that support this primary question are:

1. If Ukraine is undergoing the process of Europeanization, who is initiating the drive to Europeanize: Ukraine or the European Union?

---

[25]Münevver Cebeci and Keren raz-Netzer, "The Europeanization Process in the Mediterranean: The Case of Turkish-Israeli relations over the Last Decade," in *The European Union and the Mediterranean: The Mediterranean's European Challenge*, vol. v. (Malta: University Documentation and Research Centre, 2004): 175.

[26]Ibid. See also, Robert Ladrech, *Europeanization and National Politics* (The European Union Series) (New York: Palgrave, 2010); Ian Bache, "Europeanization: A Governance Approach," http://aei.pitt.edu/1722/ 1/Bache.pdf (accessed March 15, 2012).

[27]Ibid.

2. What concrete structural reforms toward actual Europeanization has Ukraine undertaken since 2004?

3. What is Ukraine's motivation to undergo the process of Europeanization? Is it motivated by the incentive of eventual membership in the European Union? On the other hand, if Ukraine is in fact adopting domestic reforms and institutional changes, is it because of the accepted appropriateness and legitimacy of the need for reform, and independent of the reward of future membership offered by the European Union?

Limitations of Scope

This research is limited to examining the progress of Ukraine's integration with the European Union in the years following the Orange Revolution of 2004, and the implementation of the European Union's European Neighbourhood Policy. It is a comparative case study addressing Ukraine's efforts at Europeanization in the areas of economic integration, cooperation in energy policy, and judicial reform consisting in the adaptation of Ukrainian law consistent with the *acquis communautaire* of the European Union. For the area of economic integration, this research examines the Joint European Union-Ukraine Action Plan and the European Union-Ukraine Association Agenda which have since led to the finalization, but not the signing, of an Association Agreement including a Deep and Comprehensive Free Trade Area between the European Union and Ukraine. These are respectively political and economic instruments and address various aspects of economic integration and political cooperation with the European Union. The area of energy cooperation addresses the Memorandum of Understanding on Co-operation in the Field of Energy between the European Union and Ukraine of 2005, the Agreement between the European Atomic Energy Community and the Cabinet of

Ministers of Ukraine for Co-operation in the Peaceful Uses of Nuclear Energy which entered into force in September 2006,[28] and Ukraine's recent accession to the European Energy Community to determine the extent to which Ukraine is undergoing Europeanization in its energy policy.[29] The European Union has issued a number of progress reports and annual assessments identifying the extent to which Ukraine has succeeded in implementing the terms of these agreements and thus approximating its laws to attain economic and energy standards consistent with the European Union. These reports and assessments serve as the basis for determining whether Ukraine is undertaking the process of Europeanization within its economic and energy sectors.

Finally, this research explores whether Ukraine is Europeanizing its judicial system. Since joining the Council of Europe in November 1995, Ukraine has submitted various draft legislation to the European Commission for Democracy through Law (Venice Commission). The Venice Commission, an advisory body of the Council of Europe, has provided a number of critical reports commenting on Ukraine's draft legislation and the extent to which it approximates European standards and values. The Venice Commission's reports serve as the basis to determine whether Ukraine is achieving judicial reform and thus Europeanizing its judiciary. In addition to the reports of the Venice Commission, the recent trial and conviction of Yulia Tymoshenko is of

[28] Agreement between the European Atomic Energy Community and the Cabinet of Ministers of Ukraine for Co-operation in the Peaceful Uses of Nuclear Energy, April 28, 2005, http://ec.europa.eu/world/agreements/downloadFile.do?fullText=yes&treaty TransId=10181 (accessed March 15, 2012).

[29] *Memorandum of Understanding on Co-operation in the Field of Energy between the European Union and Ukraine*, December 1, 2005, http://ec.europa.eu/dgs/energy_ transport/international/bilateral/ukraine/doc/mou_en_final_en.pdf (accessed March 15, 2012).

particular interest, raising questions of just how far Ukraine is pursuing judicial reform and whether there are limits to Ukraine's efforts at Europeanizing its judiciary.

This research adopts an analytical approach used by political scientists Frank Schimmelfennig and Ulrich Sedelmeier who examined the process of Europeanization among the Central and Eastern European countries of the 2004 Eastern enlargement.[30] Their mechanisms of Europeanization, addressed in chapter 3, describe the main elements that influence the process of Europeanization. The purpose in using Schimmelfennig's and Sedelmeier's mechanisms of Europeanization is to identify and analyze the several variables that have been important in shaping relations between the European Union and Ukraine. Much of the background material and analysis are based on the events of the last seven years of Ukrainian political and economic activities. Particularly significant is the emergence of the European Neighbourhood Policy in 2004, along with the Eastern Partnership Program in 2009. By considering recent developments in European Union-Ukraine relations, this research explores the conditions under which the European Union can promote changes at the domestic level in a European, post-Soviet state, and contributes to the ongoing debate on the influence that the European Union exerts outside its boundaries in Europe. The final objective of this thesis is to provide a set of conclusions and recommendations that may assist future readers in developing a deeper understanding of the complexities of Europeanization within the context of Ukraine-European Union relations.

---

[30]See, Frank Schimmelfennig and Ulrich Sedelmeier, eds., *The Europeanization of Central and Eastern Europe* (Ithaca: Cornell University Press, 2005).

Delimitations

This thesis does not attempt an in-depth analysis of Ukraine-European Union relations.[31] Similarly, although Russia's influence on European Union-Ukrainian relations is significant, and a factor in Ukraine's efforts at seeking increased Euro-Atlantic integration, it is nonetheless beyond the scope of this study. Scholars, such as Katarzyna Pełczyńska-Nałęcz, have been critical of the European Union's efforts at balancing relations between Russia and its Eastern neighbours.[32] There is no doubt that the European Union's relationship with Ukraine is significantly affected by its desire to maintain healthy relations with Russia, especially in the area of energy security. Russia provides approximately one quarter of the natural gas consumed in the European Union, and approximately 80 percent of those exports travel through pipelines across Ukrainian soil prior to arriving in the European Union.[33] Russia's control over vast energy resources is clearly a power tool that gives Moscow great potential to regain its status within Europe. Europe's dependency on Russia's natural gas resources is one of the few sectors enabling Russia to negotiate with Europe on an equal level. Limited mention of Russia's influence on Ukraine's efforts at economic, energy and legal reform is made throughout

---

[31]The Delegation of the European Union to Ukraine provides a comprehensive up-to-date chronology of bilateral relations complete with links to treaties and legal instruments. See, http://www.eeas.europa.eu/delegations/ukraine/eu_ukraine/chronology/index_en.htm (accessed March 15, 2012).

[32]Katarzyna Pełczyńska-Nałęcz, *Integration or Imitation?, EU Policy Towards Its Eastern Neighbours* (Warsaw: Centre for Eastern Studies, 2011), 6. See also, Marcin Łapczynski, "The European Union's Eastern Partnership: Chances and Perspectives," *Caucasian Review of International Affairs* 3, no. 2 (Spring 2009): 143-155.

[33]Olga Oliker, "Ukraine and the Caspian: An opportunity for the United States," *RAND Issue Paper* 198 (Santa Monica, CA: RAND Corporation, 2000).

this study, but only insofar as it is relevant to addressing the question of whether Ukraine is undergoing the process of Europeanization in these areas.[34]

Significance of the Study

The August 2008 conflict in Georgia underscored the need for the European Union to have a safe and secure eastern border.[35] The conflict made it clear that Russia will actively oppose western military influence on its borders, and while Moscow's opposition is aimed primarily at NATO, the Georgian conflict brought European Union-Russia relations to a new low. Arguably, the best way to keep Eastern Europe from succumbing to the increasing pressures of Russia is to ensure that countries like Ukraine undergo the process of Europeanization. Long-term stability in Europe lies in fewer barriers and the introduction of reforms in Eastern Europe aimed at securing the freedom of each state to pursue its own path as sovereign, democratic nations. Ukraine's Europeanization could foster stability in the region by removing the political and economic barriers that currently divide the countries of Eastern Europe from the European Union. If Ukraine succeeds in Europeanization and in integrating with the European Union, it could change the geopolitical dynamics in Eastern Europe and result in a westward pull on other states in the region.

---

[34]For a more comprehensive analysis of this subject see, Vsevolod Samokhvalov, "Relations in the Russia-Ukraine-EU Triangle: 'Zero-Sum Game,'" *Occasional Paper* No. 68 (Paris: European Union Institute for Security Studies, 2007), http://www.iss. europa.eu/uploads/ media/occ68.pdf (accessed March 15, 2012). See also, Licínia Simão, "Discursive Differences and Policy Outcomes: EU-Russia Relations and Security in Europe," *Eastern Journal of European Studies* 2, no. 1 (June 2011): 81-95.

[35]See, Tomas Valasek, "Why Ukraine Matters to Europe," *Centre for European Reform Essays* (London: Centre for European Reform, 2008).

The European Union considers Ukraine to be a priority partner within its European Neighbourhood Policy and Eastern Partnership Program. The prospect of European Union membership could serve as incentive to guide Ukraine as it adopts the necessary domestic changes and institutional reforms commensurate with the process of Europeanization. Moreover, Ukraine stands to have considerable influence over the other countries of Eastern Europe and the South Caucasus. Ukraine is the largest of the countries between the European Union and Russia and is positioned to set an example for countries such as Moldova and the former Soviet Republics of Armenia, Georgia and Azerbaijan. Ukraine could set the example for these countries, and ultimately perhaps even Russia, to further integrate into the global economy.

Despite the relatively intense cooperation between the European Union and Ukraine, particularly within the last seven years, Ukraine remains considerably poorer and less politically stable than the Central and Eastern European countries that joined the European Union in 2004 and 2007. While Ukraine is a democracy, confident of its European identity, the rule of law and its judicial system are arguably at odds with European Union values and norms. Moreover, Ukraine has been criticized for espousing a desire to enter the European Union, but failing to undertake concrete structural changes and reforms. This has led to ambivalence, perhaps even complacency, from the European Union as evidenced by the ambiguity of European Union External Affairs Commissioner Benita Ferrero-Waldner's statement wherein she declared that for Ukraine "nothing is ruled out and nothing is ruled in, the [European Union] door is neither open nor closed."[36] By addressing Ukraine's efforts at Europeanization this research attempts to ascertain whether bilateral relations between the European Union and Ukraine have progressed beyond this ambivalence in the years following the Orange Revolution.

Before the Orange Revolution and the implementation of the European Neighbourhood Policy, Ukraine's political leaders were often criticized for acting as though Ukraine could achieve integration simply by joining and participating in international organizational and political clubs rather than by undertaking concrete structural changes. Moreover, Ukraine appeared to be divided and ambivalent about its own foreign policy--supportive of European Union membership, but lacking the political will to pursue further integration with the European Union at the expense of upsetting its relations with Russia. Several years ago, European Union Commission President José Manuel Barroso, commenting that the onus of European integration rests with Ukraine, urged Ukraine to not talk simply about European Union membership, but instead to take concrete steps that showed a commitment to European values.[37] If it wants to achieve European Union membership, Ukraine can no longer afford to simply espouse a desire for increased European integration without engaging in a committed process of Europeanization. This research attempts to ascertain the current relations between the European Union and Ukraine and whether there has been any clarity about Ukraine's accession perspectives in the years following the Orange Revolution. Ultimately, this

---

[36]Elitsa Vucheva, "EU wants 'targeted deepening of relations' with neighbours," EUObserver.com, April 3, 2008, http://euobserver.com/15/25918 (accessed March 15, 2012).

[37]BBC News, "Ukraine told that EU door is open," October 6, 2005, http://news.bbc.co.uk/2/hi/europe/4313906.stm (accessed March 15, 2012).

research attempts to identify whether Ukraine is undertaking the process of

Europeanization and thus committing itself to a future of increasingly closer integration

with the European Union.

CHAPTER 2

LITERATURE REVIEW

This chapter introduces the literature relevant to Europeanization and the bilateral relations between the European Union and Ukraine. It highlights the current literature on the subjects of Eastern enlargement, the European Neighbourhood Policy and Eastern Partnership. The literature on Europeanization is important in order to understand the significant influence of the European Union upon a non-member state such as Ukraine. Moreover, the literature addressing Europeanization and non-member states provides context on the subject of how far and to what extent the process of Europeanization influences non-member states who aspire to European Union membership.

The process of Europeanization enjoys increasing popularity within the academic literature of European integration. Primary focus is on the literature published within the past decade, especially literature published since the emergence of the European Union's European Neighbourhood Policy. Among the many online journals dedicated to European integration, The European Community Studies Association Austria (ECSA Austria) provides one of the more comprehensive databases of publications on the subject.[38] Understanding Europeanization and the related body of literature is a critical first step to addressing the question of whether and to what extent Ukraine is Europeanizing. The intent is to understand the literature of integration theory and "the

---

[38]See, http://www2.wu-wien.ac.at/ecsa/home01en.html (accessed March 15, 2012).

sometimes confusing array of approaches that have been proliferating since the 1960s."[39]

More importantly, understanding the analytical framework of Europeanization and the

current theoretical debates aids the methodological approach used in this comparative

case study. Following a survey of the secondary literature, this chapter concludes by

identifying the significance of this present study to the existing literature.

Referring to the "mosaic of integration theory," Thomas Diez and Antje Weiner

identify three categories of European integration literature: (1) studies which address the

history of the integration process and its main actors, (2) studies which focus on the

European Union's formal institutions and particular policies, and (3) studies which deal

with present and prospective member states' policies.[40] Notwithstanding the interest that

the first two categories of literature may hold for students of European integration, they

are beyond the scope of this present study, which is limited to addressing Ukrainian

policies and programs within the context of European Union-Ukrainian bilateral

relations. Although Ukraine is not a candidate for membership in the European Union,[41]

the literature within this third category, particularly the 2004/2007 Eastern enlargement,

is relevant since it outlines the measures adopted by present and prospective member

---

[39]Antje Wiener and Thomas Diez, eds., *European Integration Theory*, 2d. ed., (Oxford: Oxford University Press, 2009), 1. "This is a booming field, and readers will know better than anyone else the difficulties in choosing the appropriate literature." Ibid.

[40]Ibid.

[41]The five candidate countries who have applied to the European Union and have been accepted in principle are: Iceland, Macedonia, Montenegro, Serbia and Turkey. See, European Commission, Enlargement, http://ec.europa.eu/enlargement/index_ en.htm (accessed March 15, 2012).

states in their efforts to attain the Copenhagen Criteria[42] by undertaking the process of Europeanization.[43] Because Ukraine does not hold official candidate status, the literature of European Union-Ukrainian relations is most often written in terms of European integration, with less emphasis and use of the term Europeanization. Nonetheless, because the European Union and Ukraine are seeking an increasingly closer relationship, and the fact that Ukraine is a priority partner within the Eastern Partnership, it is certainly valid to speak of European Union-Ukrainian relations in terms of Europeanization.

<u>Europeanization and the Bi-lateral Relations between
the European Union and Ukraine</u>

European integration encompasses the political, economic, legal, social and cultural integration of states geographically located wholly or partially in Europe. There are a number of book-length studies and scholarly articles on the history of European integration. Two of the better introductions on this subject are Andrew Moravcsik's, *The*

---

[42]"Membership requires that candidate country has achieved stability of institutions guaranteeing democracy, the rule of law, human rights, respect for and protection of minorities, the existence of a functioning market economy as well as the capacity to cope with competitive pressure and market forces within the Union. Membership presupposes the candidate's ability to take on the obligations of membership including adherence to the aims of political, economic and monetary union." The European Council articulated the criteria specifically in relation to the countries of Central and Eastern Europe as part of the 2004/2007 Enlargement. See, Presidency Conclusions, Copenhagen European Council--21-22 June 1993, http://www.europarl. europa.eu/enlargement/ec/pdf/cop_en.epdf (accessed March 15, 2012).

[43]A representative example of this type of literature is Frank Schimmelfennig and Ulrich Sedelmeier, eds., *The Europeanization of Central and Eastern Europe* (Ithaca: Cornell University Press, 2005).

Choice for Europe[44] published in 1998, and the more recent *Ever Closer Union,* by

Desmond Dinan.[45] Placing less emphasis on national security concerns, Moravcsik sees

economic interdependence among the European governments as the primary force

compelling states to coordinate core economic policies and to seek increased political

integration. Similarly, Dinan's work discusses how European Union member

governments have chosen closer union in order to promote their countries' economic

interests. These studies are relevant to current European Union-Ukraine relations since

they provide a framework in which to understand the recent negotiations which have

since led to the drafting of an Association Agreement and Deep and Comprehensive Free

Trade Area between the European Union and Ukraine.

Related to studies on European integration are those addressing the process of

Europeanization. Despite considerable debate about how to define Europeanization,

scholars generally use the term as shorthand for "influence of the European Union" or

"domestic impact of the European Union." Europeanization does not eliminate

established national structures and practices; it requires a degree of internalization of

European values and policy paradigms at the domestic level.[46] In his article on the

subject of enlargement, particularly within the European Neighbourhood Policy, Amichai

---

[44]Andrew Moravcsik, *The Choice for Europe: social purpose & state power from Messina to Maastricht*, Cornell Studies in Political Economy (Ithaca: Cornell University Press, 1998).

[45]Desmond Dinan, *Ever Closer Union: an introduction to European integration*, 4th ed. (Boulder, CO: Lynne Rienner, 2010). See also, Desmond Dinan, ed., *Origins and Evolution of the European Union,* The New European Union Series (Oxford: Oxford University Press, 2006).

[46]See Johan P. Olsen, "The Many Faces of Europeanization," *Journal of Common Market Studies* 40, no. 5 (2002): 921-52.

Magen explores the effects of Europeanization, or what is sometimes referred to as "EU-ization," and "the diffusion of formal and informal rules, procedures, practices, and beliefs that are first defined in European Union policy processes and then incorporated into the domestic (national and sub-national) structures, policies, and identities of member states."[47]

In their article on Europeanization in Hungary and Ukraine, Melinda Kovács and Olena Leipnik distinguish between Europeanization as a process and as a concept.[48] The process of Europeanization is practical, i.e. institutional transformation, whereas the concept of Europeanization is more ideological.[49] Europeanization as a process is the focus of most of the literature on Europeanization. Among the works that assume the process of Europeanization, several view it as a synonym for processes of approaching the European Union. For example, Michael Baun *et al.* write about the Czech Republic and how its politics and party system were "Europeanized" prior to its 2004 accession.[50] Carlos Mendez *et al.* focus on how competition and cohesion policies are negotiated

---

[47]Amichai Magen, "The Shadow of Enlargement: Can the European Neighbour-hood Policy Achieve Compliance?" *The Columbia Journal of European Law* 12, no. 2 (Spring 2006): 384-427, 385. On legal and institutional aspects of Europeanization, see generally Francis Snyder, ed., *The Europeanization of Law: The Legal Effects of European Integration* (Oxford: Hart Publishing, 2005); Maria Green Cowles, James Caporaso and Thomas Risse, eds., *Transforming Europe: Europeani-zation and Domestic Change* (Ithaca: Cornell University, 2001).

[48]Melinda Kovács and Olena Leipnik, "The Borders of Orientalism: "Europeani-zation" in Hungary and Ukraine," *Debatte* 16, no. 2 (August 2008): 151-169, 156.

[49]Ibid., 151.

[50]Michael Baun, Jakub Dürr, Dan Marek, and Pavel Saradin, "The Europeani-zation of Czech Politics: The Political Parties and the EU Referendum," *Journal of Common Market Studies* 44, no. 2 (2006): 249–80.

between the European Union and its member states. Their work uses the term Europeanization to mean synchronizing policies within the European Union.[51]

Kovács' and Leipnik's distinction between Europeanization as a process and a concept is relevant to understanding Europeanization in Ukraine, albeit in a somewhat pessimistic sense. The authors suggest that Ukrainians lack "a clear understanding of what Europe itself is, not to mention more detailed knowledge of European institutions." They point out that a distorted understanding of Europeanization "engenders inferiorization and self-inferiorization" in societies such as Ukraine where an appearance of "Europeanization" is occurring, as opposed to true institutional development.[52]

> The process that is going on in Ukraine under the name of "Europeanization" can be seen as a simulation . . . The real content of the idea of "Europeanization" is not clear for many (if not most) Ukrainians; however, the word is used by politicians as a key characteristic and the main priority of strategic goals for the development of the country.[53]

Kovács' and Leipnik's treatment of Europeanization as an institutional process and a concept is relevant to Ukraine and the validity of the distinction, particularly whether the concept "engenders inferiorization," is addressed more fully in chapter 4.

Arista Maria Cirtautas and Frank Schimmelfennig identify two strands in the literature on the enlargement policy of the European Union.[54] The first explains why the

---

[51]Carlos Mendez, Fiona Wishlade and Douglas Yuill, "Conditioning and Fine-tuning Europeanization: Negotiating Regional Policy Maps under the EU's Competition and Cohesion Policies," *Journal of Common Market Studies* 44, no. 3 (2006): 581-605.

[52]Kovács and Leipnik, "The Borders of Orientalism," 152, 158.

[53]Ibid., 158.

[54]Arista Maria Cirtautas and Frank Schimmelfennig, "Europeanisation Before and After Accession: Conditionality, Legacies and Compliance," *Europe-Asia Studies* 62, no. 3 (May 2010): 421–441, 422.

European Union expanded into Central and Eastern Europe, selecting some Eastern

European countries as candidates and not others.[55] A second body of literature focuses on

the Europeanization process that occurred within the countries of Central and Eastern

Europe, "including the transfer of European Union norms and rules to the accession

countries, and the conditions under which they have adopted and complied with these

norms and rules."[56]

Cirtautas and Schimmelfennig outline three approaches within the literature of the

European Union's Eastern Enlargement. First, they cite the theory of Liberal

Intergovernmentalism, developed by Andrew Moravcsik, which assumes that states are

actors. The European Union, as an actor, achieves its goals through intergovernmental

negotiation and bargaining, and not through centralized authority making or the

enforcement of political decisions.[57] Moravscik's theory points out that most of the

policy issues of the European Union are economic and that the "prospect of internal

warfare among democratic capitalist states is remote."[58] Therefore the "preferences of

---

[55]See, Frank Schimmelfennig and Ulrich Sedelmeier, eds., *The Politics of European Union Enlargement: Theoretical Approaches* (London: Routledge, 2005).

[56]See, Frank Schimmelfennig and Ulrich Sedelmeier, "Candidate Countries and Conditionality" in P. Graziano and M. Vink, eds., *Europeanization: New Research Agendas* (Basingstoke: Palgrave Macmillan, 2007); Ulrich Sedelmeier, "Europeanisation in New Member and Candidate States," *Living Reviews in European Governance* 6, no. 1 (2011): 3, http://www.livingreviews.org/lreg-2011-1 (accessed March 15, 2012).

[57]See, Andrew Moravcsik and Frank Schimmelfennig, "Liberal Intergovern-mentalism," in Wiener and Diez, eds., *European Integration Theory*, 67-87. "The European Union "is best seen as an international regime for policy co-ordination." Ibid., 68, citing Andrew Moravcsik, "Preferences and Power in the European Community: A Liberal Intergovernmentalist Approach," *Journal of Common Market Studies* 31, no. 4 (December 1993), 473-524, 480.

[58]Ibid., 70.

national governments regarding European integration have mainly reflected concrete economic interests rather than other general concerns like security or European ideals."[59] Moravcsik's, *The Choice of Europe,* frames European Union integration within the theory of Liberal Intergovernmentalism:

> European Union integration can best be understood as a series of rational choices made by national leaders. These choices responded to constraints and opportunities stemming from the economic interests of powerful domestic constituents, the relative power of states stemming from asymmetrical interdependence, and the role of institutions in bolstering the credibility of interstate commitments.[60]

Under this theory, state preferences and bargaining power explain the European Union's decision to expand in Central and Eastern Europe. Another way of looking at these assumptions which informs Liberal Intergovernmentalism is a three-stage framework focusing on "precise theories of preferences, bargaining, and institutionalization."[61] A state defines its preferences, bargains with other states for substantive gains guaranteed in agreements, and ultimately creates or amends its institutions "to secure those outcomes in the face of future uncertainty."[62] This three-stage framework is used to frame the issue of whether Ukraine is undertaking the process of Europeanization. Applying Liberal Intergovernmentalism to the European Union's position vis-à-vis Ukraine suggests that the two will pursue an intensive policy of cooperation and increased integration because of shared interests, particularly in the realm of economics.

---

[59]Ibid. "National security is not the dominant motivation" driving European integration.

[60]Andrew Moravscik, *The Choice for Europe*, 18.

[61]Moravcsik and Schimmelfennig, "Liberal Intergovernmentalism," in Wiener and Diez, *European Integration Theory*, 68.

[62]Ibid., 68-69.

A second approach within the context of enlargement and Europeanization focuses on geopolitics and is best expressed by L.S. Skålnes, in his chapter, "Geopolitics and the Eastern Enlargement of the European Union."[63] The geopolitical explanation emphasizes security rather than commercial and financial interests as the prime motivation behind enlargement and Europeanization.

Ideational or constructivist explanations of enlargement represent the third approach within the literature of the European Union's Eastern enlargement policy. These explanations focus on "constructions of European Union identity and European Union norms" and are based on "legacies of European Union policy that created an obligation to admit ex-communist countries."[64] For example, K.M. Fierke and A. Wiener address European Union Eastern enlargement policy as a legacy of "the Western promise of inclusion and support for reform during the Cold War."[65] Ulrich Sedelmeier writes of the European Union's "special responsibility" vis-à-vis the countries of Eastern Europe following the collapse of communism.[66] Cirtautas and Schimmelfennig stress that

---

[63]See, L.S. Skålnes, "Geopolitics and the Eastern Enlargement of the European Union," in *The Politics of European Union Enlargement: Theoretical Approaches,* ed. Frank Schimmelfennig and Ulrich Sedelmeier (London: Routledge, 2005): 213-233.

[64]Cirtautas and Schimmelfennig, "Europeanisation Before and After Accession," 424.

[65]K.M. Fierke and A. Wiener, "Constructing Institutional Interests: EU and NATO Enlargement," *Journal of European Public Policy* 6, no. 5 (December 1999).

[66]Ulrich Sedelmeier, "Eastern Enlargement: Risk, Rationality, and Role-Compliance," in *Risks, Reforms, Resistance and Revival* 5 of *The State of the European Union*, ed. Maria Green Cowles and Michael Smith (Oxford: Oxford University Press, 2000): 164-185. See also, Ulrich Sedelmeier, *Constructing the Path to Eastern Enlargement: The Uneven Policy Impact of EU Identity* (Manchester: Manchester University Press, 2005).

ideational or constructivist explanations emphasize "current achievements in liberal democratic reform and consolidation" within Central and Eastern Europe, rather than on their history.[67]

Related to ideational or constructivist explanations of enlargement is the body of literature which addresses the Europeanization of Central and Eastern Europe within the context of the "interplay of contemporary international and domestic conditions."[68] Frank Schimmelfennig and Ulrich Sedelmeier have developed explanatory mechanisms to account for the process of Europeanization among the Central and Eastern European countries of the 2004 Eastern enlargement. Schimmelfennig's and Sedelmeier's "external incentives model" offers perhaps the best overall explanation in support of the Europeanization of the Central and Eastern European countries of the 2004 Eastern enlargement. This model "suggests that the adoption of democratic and human rights norms as well as European Union legal norms depends on the size and credibility of tangible, material incentives."[69] Schimmelfennig and Sedelmeier emphasize the prospect of European Union membership rather than communist or pre-communist legacies as the motivation which spurred Central and Eastern European governments to undertake the process of Europeanization. Schimmelfennig and Sedelmeier offer two alternative

---

[67]Cirtautas and Schimmelfennig, "Europeanisation Before and After Accession," 424.

[68]Ibid.

[69]See generally, Schimmelfennig and Sedelmeier, eds., *The Europeanization of Central and Eastern Europe*; Frank Schimmelfennig and Ulrich Sedelmeier, "Governance by Conditionality: EU Rule Transfer to the Candidate Countries of Central and Eastern Europe," *Journal of European Public Policy* 11, no. 4 (August 2004); Ulrich Sedelmeier, "After Conditionality: Post-Accession Compliance with EU Law in East Central Europe," *Journal of European Public Policy* 15, no. 6 (September 2008).

explanations supporting the process of Europeanization: "social learning" and "lesson drawing" models. Both focus on the legitimacy of European Union rules and policies and the "contemporary identification of the governments and societies" of Central and Eastern Europe with the Western European international community that is the European Union.[70] Although the authors do not address European countries outside those of the 2004 enlargement, their theoretical approach and methodology is relevant to addressing the matter of whether Ukraine is undertaking the process of Europeanization. Their theoretical approach and methodology, particularly the explanatory mechanisms used to account for the process of Europeanization, serve as the basis for the methodology of this present research and are discussed more fully in chapter 3.

Annette Elisabeth Töller describes Europeanization as "the process in which certain institutionalized aspects of government and administrative cultures of the member states change as a result of European Union-level policies."[71] In other words, Europeanization is "the impact that European policies in particular and European integration in general have on national polities, politics and policies."[72] Notwithstanding the lack of official candidate status or open negotiations with the European Union, a non-member state may choose to adopt a policy of Europeanization. A European state that

---

[70]Cirtautas and Schimmelfennig, "Europeanisation Before and After Accession," 424. In this perspective, the 'Return to Europe' is a reaction to the end of communism and Soviet hegemony and an expression of normative realignment in a changed political environment.

[71]Annette Elisabeth Töller, "The Europeanization of Public Policies--Understanding Idiosyncratic Mechanisms and Contingent Results," *European Integration Online Papers* 8, no. 9 (2004), http://econpapers.repec.org/article/erpeiopxx/p0114. htm (accessed March 15, 2012).

[72]Ibid.

aspires to membership within the European Union need not have applied for membership or wait for the initiation of formal negotiations in order to begin the process of Europeanization.[73] This is somewhat related to "anticipatory adaptation," in which a non-member state adopts European Union rules in anticipation of membership requirements. For example, Liliana B. Andonova has written about Poland's process of Europeanization which started as early as 1989-1990, with its adoption of European Union standards of environmental regulation, several years before the European Commission extended an invitation to begin negotiations.[74] The first post-communist government in Poland adopted a National Environmental Program in 1990 in an effort to strengthen environmental protection, and adopted a series of economic incentives aimed at reducing air emissions within the energy sector. Poland's initiative to Europeanize its environmental policy predates the initiation of its negotiations for European Union accession. Not until the Luxembourg summit in 1997, did the European Union accept the European Commission's opinion to invite several Central and Eastern European states, including Poland, to initiate talks on their accession to the European Union. The negotiation process for Poland started on March 31, 1998. Andonova addresses a similar process of voluntary Europeanization occurred within the Czech Republic.[75]

---

[73]See, Stephen Haggard et al., "Integrating the Two Halves of Europe: Theories of Interests, Bargaining, and Institutions," in *After the Cold War: International Institutions and State Strategies in Europe 1989-1991*, ed. Robert O. Keohane, Joseph S. Nye and Stanley Hoffmann (Cambridge: Harvard University Press, 1993): 173-195.

[74]See, Liliana B. Andonova, "The Europeanization of Environmental Policy in the Czech Republic and Poland," in Schimmelfennig and Sedelmeier, *The Europeanization of Central and Eastern Europe*.

[75]Ibid.

How may a candidate state, or for that matter, a non-candidate state such as Ukraine, undertake the process of Europeanization? Christopher Knill and Dirk Lehmkuhl identify three mechanisms in the process of Europeanization. The first mechanism concerns institutional compliance. It is prescriptive; the European Union requires a prospective state to adopt specific measures, adjusting its domestic policies with limited domestic institutional discretion.[76] This mechanism is most evident in the "Copenhagen Criteria" established at a June 1993 meeting of the European Council and which require that a state has the institutions to preserve democratic governance and human rights, a functioning market economy, and accepts the obligations and intent of the European Union. A second mechanism concerns the impact of European Union legislation which "alters the distribution of power and resources" and "requires institutional change."[77] The third mechanism of Europeanization involves the "shaping [of] domestic beliefs and expectations" to strengthen support for "broader European reform objectives" which in turn leads to institutional adaptation. [78]

In recent years, prominent Ukrainian political and business leaders, public figures, scientists and intellectuals have frequently voiced support for Ukraine's "European choice." For example, Volodymyr Stretovych, member of Ukraine's Parliament, and Head of the Committee on the Struggle Against Organized Crime and Corruption, sees Ukraine's European integration as the "restoration of historical justice"--a "return to the

---

[76]See, Christoph Knill and Dirk Lehmkuhl, "How Europe Matters: Different Mechanisms of Europeanization," European Integration Online Papers 3, no. 7 (1999), 6-7, http://econpapers.repec.org/ article/erpeiopxx/p0040.htm (accessed March 15, 2012).

[77]Knill and Lehmkuhl, "How Europe Matters," 7.

[78]Ibid.

bosom of the family of European nations, where it was a thousand years ago."[79] Oleh Samchyshyn, President of Ukraine's Consumer Association, views European integration in more specific terms: "'Ukraine's European choice' is a market economy, democracy, principles of equal rights and equal starting opportunities for every person in Ukraine."[80] Myroslav Popovych, Director of the Institute for Philosophy, National Academy of Science of Ukraine, offered perhaps the strongest support for European integration when he remarked that Ukraine's failure to integrate into Europe would result in a "state of ideological isolation" for Ukraine.[81]

James Sherr, currently Senior Fellow of the Russia and Eurasia Programme at the Royal Institute of International Affairs, Chatham House, offers a critical perspective on Ukraine's approach to European integration. Writing in 1998, Sherr remarked that "Ukraine's political leaders have sometimes acted as if they could achieve integration by declaration, or simply by joining and participating in international organizational and political clubs rather than by undertaking concrete structural changes."[82] Sherr's

---

[79]Center for Peace, Conversion and Foreign Policy of Ukraine, "European Integration of Ukraine as Viewed by Top Ukrainian Politicians, Businessmen and Society Leaders" (Warsaw: Center for Peace, Conversion and Foreign Policy of Ukraine, 2003), 30, 23-24.

[80]Ibid., 22-23.

[81]Ibid., 21. "Ukraine's failure to join the cultural-political and financial-economic Europe, but a competitive Eurasian centre with Russia in its heart will inevitably turn Ukraine into a half-European province of an eastern neighbour."

[82]James Sherr, *Ukraine's New Time of Troubles*, Institut for Forsvarsstudier, ISO Info 6/1998 (Oslo: Norwegian Institute for Defence Studies, 1998), 11, http://www. ifspublications.com/ (accessed March 15, 2012). Sherr served as a Fellow at the Advanced Research Assessment Group and Conflict Studies Research Centre, Royal Military Academy, 1995-2008.

perspective remains relevant; Ukraine's political elites continue to issue foreign policy declarations expressing a willingness to participate in European integration particularly through membership in the European Union. Despite the rhetoric, however, there is the question of whether Ukraine is adopting necessary domestic reforms and changes to its institutions and policies consistent with those of the European Union. The question is not whether Ukraine is a part of Europe, but whether Ukraine has a realistic chance of claiming membership in the European Union in the foreseeable future by embracing the process of Europeanization. Notwithstanding the declarations in support of Ukraine's "European choice," the country's elite still has to deliver policies supportive of the actual movement toward liberal democracy and a functioning market economy.

In her 2004 European University Institute working paper, Kataryna Wolczuk, currently Deputy Director of the Centre for Russian and East European Studies, University of Birmingham, sought to explain why the progress of Ukraine's integration with the European Union had been confined to the rhetoric of foreign policy declarations.[83] Wolczuk found that Ukraine sought integration with the European Union, but was unable to enact domestic reforms consistent with the process of Europeanization. Her thesis is all the more significant since she was writing at a time when Ukraine's Central and Eastern European neighbours--Poland, Slovakia and Hungary--successfully implemented domestic reforms sufficient to earn membership in the European Union. Wolczuk found that at the time of her research, Ukraine remained "simultaneously divided and ambivalent about foreign policy" and that while it was largely supportive of

---

[83]Kataryna Wolczuk, "Integration without Europeanisation: Ukraine and its Policy towards the European Union," European Union Institute Working Papers, RSCAS No. 2004/15 (Florence, Italy: Robert Schuman Centre for Advanced Studies, 2004): 1-22.

European Union membership, its political elites did not face "societal pressure for pursuing this particular foreign policy option."[84] Although the benefits of participation in European integration were not lost on its political elites, she found that merely seeking European integration through foreign policy instruments, such as the Partnership and Cooperation Agreement, had not actually fostered domestic and institutional reforms. She concluded her study by characterizing Ukraine's policy towards the European Union as one of integration without Europeanization.[85]

Wolczuk noted further in her 2004 study that there was "little literature on Europeanisation in non-prospective member states in Europe."[86] She believed this was due to the European Union largely neglecting countries like Ukraine, Moldova and Belarus in its external policy, and the "perceived intractability of their post-Soviet transformations."[87] The European Neighbourhood Policy of 2004 and subsequent Eastern Partnership of 2009 have since signaled the European Union's new approach in relations with its Eastern European neighbours. Scholars have been critical of Eastern Partnership, however, arguing the initiative has been developed largely by the European Union, rather than with the joint participation of the countries that make up Eastern Partnership. In addition to an introductory overview of the policy's main features, Whitman's and

---

[84]Ibid., 21.

[85]Ibid., 22.

[86]Ibid., 2.

[87]Ibid.

Wolff's, *The European Neighbourhood Policy in Perspective,*[88] highlights the challenges

of implementing the program. Among the articles in this collection is Gwendolyn Sasse's

study of Moldova and Ukraine as test cases for assessing the implementation and impact

of the European Neighbourhood Policy.[89] Elena Korosteleva has written a critical

assessment of the development and impact of the European Neighbourhood Policy and

the Eastern Partnership on its eastern neighbours--Belarus, Ukraine and Moldova in

particular--in an attempt to understand advantages and problems related to the effective

implementation of European Union policies in the eastern region.[90]

There is a growing body of literature assessing the impact of the European

Neighbourhood Policy and Eastern Partnership within Ukraine since the publication of

Wolczuk's 2004 study. Following its annual conference in Kyiv in October 2006, the

University of Sussex European Institute's Wider Europe Programme published a

collection of essays on the European Neighbourhood Policy and Ukraine.[91] Two of the

essays bear directly on the research for this current study: Roman Petrov's "Past and

---

[88]Richard G. Whitman and Stefan Wolff, eds., *The European Neighbourhood Policy in Perspective: Context, Implementation and Impact*, Palgrave Studies in European Union Politics (New York: Palgrave Macmillan, 2009).

[89]Gwendolyn Sasse, "The ENP and the EU's Eastern Neighbours: Ukraine and Moldova as Test Cases," 182-205.

[90]Elena Korosteleva, ed., *Eastern Partnership: A New Opportunity for the Neighbours?* (London: Routledge, 2011).

[91]Nathaniel Copsey and Alan Mayhew, eds., "European Neighbourhood Policy: the Case of Ukraine," *Sussex European Institute Seminar Papers Series*, No. 1 (January 2007) www.sei.ac.uk (accessed March 15, 2012).

Future Action on Approximation of Ukrainian Legislation to that of the EU,"[92] and

"Ukraine's Economy and EU Integration" by Igor Burakovsky, Andrii Goncharuk and

Alan Mayhew.[93] Laure Delcour's article, "Does the European Neighbourhood Policy

make a difference,"[94] written in 2007, is an early assessment of the policy's public

perception in Ukraine and Russia. In addition to her 2004 European University Institute

working paper, "Integration without Europeanisation," Wolczuk has published two

additional studies critical of the European Neighbourhood Policy: "Adjectival

Europeanisation? The Impact of EU Conditionality on Ukraine under the European

Neighbourhood Policy,"[95] and "Implementation without Coordination: The Impact of EU

Conditionality on Ukraine under the European Neighbourhood Policy."[96]

In her April 2011 study of the European Union's policy of integration towards its

Eastern neighbours, Katarzyna Pełczyńska-Nałęcz of Warsaw's Centre for Eastern

Studies questions whether Eastern Partnership has any chance of success.

---

[92]Roman Petrov's "Past and Future Action on Approximation of Ukrainian Legislation to that of the EU," in ibid.

[93]Igor Burakovsky, Andrii Goncharuk and Alan Mayhew, "Ukraine's Economy and EU Integration," in ibid.

[94]Laure Delcour, "Does the European Neighbourhood Policy Make a Difference? Policy Patterns and Reception in Ukraine and Russia," *European Political Economy Review*, Special Issue No. 7 (Summer 2007): 118-155.

[95]Kataryna Wolczuk, "Adjectival Europeanisation? The Impact of EU Conditionality on Ukraine under the European Neighbourhood Policy," *European Research Working Paper Series*, Number 18, August 2007, http://www.eri.bham.ac.uk/ research/working_papers/ WP18Wolczuk.pdf (accessed March 15, 2012).

[96]Kataryna Wolczuk, "Implementation without Coordination: The Impact of EU Conditionality on Ukraine under the European Neighbourhood Policy," *Europe-Asia Studies* 61, no. 2 (2009): 187-211.

Acknowledging that "Eastern Europe's convergence to European Union standards in political and economic terms is an enormous challenge," she questions whether the European Union sees integration with its Eastern neighbours "as an issue important enough to warrant investing significant resources in this process," particularly at a time when the European Union is beset with what she sees as "political and bureaucratic inertia."[97] Part of her study addresses what she sees as the "dilemma" of the European Union's policy towards its eastern neighbours. For example, in promoting its values, the European Union appears "unable to resolve the dilemma of whether it should condemn authoritarian tendencies and support grassroots democratic movements" or whether it should simply "choose stability and the economic benefits resulting from trade cooperation with Eastern European governments (regardless of their attitude to democracy)."[98] Much of the apparent dilemma, however, may be explained by the European Union's balancing act as it attempts to foster increased European integration among its eastern neighbours such as Moldova and Ukraine, while avoiding any confrontation with Russia. It is significant that in January 2009, just a few months before the European Union launched its Eastern Partnership, a number of disputes between Ukrainian oil and gas company Naftogaz Ukrainy and Russian gas supplier Gazprom

---

[97]Katarzyna Pełczyńska-Nałęcz, *Integration or Imitation? EU Policy towards its Eastern Neighbours* (Warsaw: Centre for Eastern Studies, 2011), 6. See also, Marcin Łapczynski, "The European Union's Eastern Partnership: Chances and Perspectives," *Caucasian Review of International Affairs* 3, no. 2 (Spring 2009): 143-155.

[98]Ibid., 11.

over natural gas supplies, prices, and debts, resulted in Russia disrupting its gas supplies to some eighteen European countries.[99]

Iryna Solonenko's article, "External Democracy Promotion in Ukraine: The Role of the European Union," explores the limited role which the European Union has thus far played in promoting democracy in Ukraine.[100] Solonenko argues that in the early 1990s, the European Union chose not to treat Ukraine as one of the Central and East European countries, which determined the subsequent ambiguity of Ukraine's orientation. As a consequence, a "Russia-first" policy persisted in Ukraine for a long time. Solonenko concludes her study by suggesting that because the European Union failed to make its policy values-based, the impact of the European Union on Ukraine will remain limited.

Among the more significant efforts of the European Neighbourhood Policy have been the negotiations of an Association Agenda between the European Union and Ukraine beginning in 2009. These negotiations have since led to the drafting of an Association Agreement encompassing a Deep and Comprehensive Free Trade Area (DCFTA), both of which were finalized in December 2011, but have yet to be signed. Roman Petrov's, "Legal Basis and Scope of the New EU-Ukraine Enhanced Agreement"[101] is an early study of the strategic importance underpinning the European

---

[99]See, Oleksandr Sushko, Iulian Chifu, and Oazu Nantoi, *Russia-Ukraine 2009 Gas Crisis: Comparative view from Kyiv, Bucharest and Chisinau*, (Kyiv: Institute for Euro-Atlantic Cooperation, 2010), http://www.cpc-ew.ro/pdfs/gaz_book.pdf (accessed March 15, 2012).

[100]Iryna Solonenko, "External Democracy Promotion in Ukraine: the role of the European Union," *Democratization* 16, no. 4 (2009): 709-731.

[101]Roman Petrov, "Legal Basis and Scope of the New EU-Ukraine Enhanced Agreement. Is there any room for further speculation?" *Max Weber Programme Working*

Union and Ukrainian trade relations. Michael Emerson, Project Director at the Centre for European Policy Studies, Brussels, compiled a lengthy and comprehensive study entitled "The Prospect of Deep Free Trade between the European Union and Ukraine," in 2006.[102] Commissioned by the European Commission as part of the European Union-Ukraine Action Plan of 2004, the study served as the basis for developing the content and economic implications of the free trade agreement which has since been finalized in the DCFTA. The DCFTA and its significance in terms of Ukraine's efforts to seek increased economic integration with the European Union is discussed more fully in chapter 4.

<u>Significance of Thesis in Relation to Existing Literature</u>

This literature review serves as a starting point for understanding the subjects of European integration and Europeanization and the recent history and significance of European Union-Ukraine relations. The years preceding the Orange Revolution of 2004 and the European Union's European Neighbourhood Policy brought forth relatively scant literature on the relationship between Ukraine and the European Union. James Sherr's 1998 study, *Ukraine's New Time of Troubles*, correctly assessed Ukraine's efforts to Europeanize as amounting to little more than simply joining and participating in international organizational and political clubs without undertaking concrete structural changes that would have brought Ukraine closer to European Union norms and values.

Papers, European University Institute, 2008, http://cadmus.eui.eu/dspace/handle/ 1814/8709 (accessed March 15, 2012).

[102]Michael Emerson, comp., *The Prospect of Deep Free Trade between the European Union and Ukraine, Centre For European Policy Studies, Brussels*, 2006, http://www.ceps.be (accessed March 15, 2012). The authors assisting in the project were a group of European Union and Ukrainian economists.

Similarly, Kataryna Wolczuk's 2004 study for the European University Institute characterized Ukraine's policy toward the European Union as one of integration without Europeanization. Wolczuk found Ukraine to be largely supportive of European Union membership, but remarked that "[d]espite numerous declarations by Ukrainian foreign policy officials in external fora, [Ukraine's] 'European choice' barely features in the domestic political debate and does not inform policy-making in Kyiv. This is because even though few are overtly opposed to it, it lacks staunch support of key political actors and the bureaucracy."[103] Her remarks reflect the general ambivalence characteristic of Ukraine's political elites at the turn of the millennium, many of whom frequently declared public support for Ukraine's European integration, but failed to initiate significant domestic reforms or pursue a more assertive relationship with the European Union despite a Ukrainian populace increasingly supportive of European integration.

This research attempts to fill a gap in the literature following Wolczuk's 2004 study. It attempts to examine the progress of Ukraine's integration with the European Union since 2004 in an effort to determine whether Wolczuk's assessment of Ukraine's policy toward the European Union--integration without Europeanization--remains valid today. In addition to contributing to the literature on Europeanization and European Union-Ukraine relations, this research adds to the growing literature that addresses the conditions under which the European Union influences institutions and policies among non-member states.

---

[103] Wolczuk, "Integration without Europeanisation," 8.

CHAPTER 3

METHODOLOGY

This chapter introduces explanatory mechanisms of Europeanization and

describes the methodology used in this research to assess whether Ukraine is undergoing

the process of Europeanization. In addition, relying on the explanatory mechanisms and

applying the methodology should identify not only whether the European Union or

Ukraine is initiating the process of Europeanization, but also assist in determining the

character of Ukraine's approach to Europeanization. For example, is Ukraine undertaking

the process of Europeanization because of identifiable rewards or incentives offered by

the European Union, or is Ukraine adopting European Union laws and policies simply

because of their perceived legitimacy and appropriateness?

This is a comparative case study addressing three areas: economic integration,

energy cooperation and judicial reform. Primary source material derives from official

agreements, annual progress reports and studies issued by the European Commission, the

Government of Ukraine and the Council of Europe. In addition, the European Union

External Action Service provides all relevant source material pertaining to the European

Neighbourhood Policy and Eastern Partnership, including bilateral agreements, policy

reports, implementation assessments and press announcements.[104] The Ministry of

---

[104]See, http://www.europa.eu (accessed March 15, 2012). Europa.eu is the official website of the European Union and the best starting point for information and services provided by the European Union. The website for the European Union External Action Service provides information about the European Neighbourhood Policy, http://eeas.europa.eu/enp/index_en.htm (accessed March 15, 2012). See also, eastbook.eu, a website dedicated to publishing information about the European Union's Eastern Partnership, http.eastbook.eu (accessed March 15, 2012).

Foreign Affairs for Ukraine provides similar materials on the bilateral relations between the European Union and Ukraine.[105] This chapter outlines the explanatory mechanisms of Europeanization and then addresses the methodology used to evaluate the source materials. After describing the research methodology, this chapter concludes with a brief discussion of the strengths and weaknesses of the selected methodology.

This research adopts the explanatory mechanisms of Europeanization identified by Frank Schimmelfennig, professor of European politics at the Center for Comparative and International Studies at the Swiss Federal Institute of Technology in Zurich, Switzerland.[106] His work in comparative and international studies includes European integration theory and the politics of enlargement of the European Union. Schimmelfennig collaborated with Ulrich Sedelmeier and edited a series of case studies investigating and assessing the domestic impact of European Union membership on the then-candidate countries of Central and Eastern Europe in the years immediately preceding the 2004 Eastern enlargement.[107] Their research examined the conditions under which the Central and Eastern European candidate countries undertook the process of Europeanization, which they define as the process by which states adopt European Union rules. This research applies their explanatory mechanisms of Europeanization to Ukraine.

---

[105]See, http://www.mfa.gov.ua (accessed March 15, 2012).

[106]See, official site of the Swiss Federal Institute of Technology, http://www.eup. ethz.ch (accessed March 16, 2012).

[107]Schimmelfennig and Sedelmeier, eds., *The Europeanization of Central and Eastern Europe*.

There are four explanatory mechanisms for Europeanization: conditionality, socialization, externalization and imitation.[108] Second, there are two key distinctions in the process of Europeanization: (1) Europeanization can be initiated either by the European Union or the individual non-member state, and (2) Europeanization can follow either a "logic of consequences" or a "logic of appropriateness."[109] A non-member state such as Ukraine may undertake the process of Europeanization based on certain conditions or rewards, for example the promise of financial support and technical assistance, or full membership within the European Union ("logic of consequences"); or a state may choose to adopt European Union rules because it is convinced of the legitimacy of the rules and appropriateness of the behavior ("logic of appropriateness"). The four mechanisms of Europeanization are divided between two logical courses of action: conditionality and externalization follow a "logic of consequences" model; socialization and imitation follow a "logic of appropriateness" model. The following table, adapted from the work of Schimmelfennig and Sedelmeier,[110] depicts the mechanisms used in this research.

---

[108]Schimmelfennig and Sedelmeier characterize externalization and imitation as "lesson-drawing" models. See, Frank Schimmelfennig, "Europeanisation Beyond the Member States," *Zeitschrift für Staats- und Europawissenschaften* 8, no. 3 (2010): 319-339. English manuscript version available at: http://www.eup.ethz.ch/people/ schimmelfennig/publications/ 10_ZSE_Europeanization__manuscript_.pdf (accessed March 16, 2012).

[109]Schimmelfennig and Sedelmeier, eds., *The Europeanization of Central and Eastern Europe*, 8-9. See also James March and Johan Olsen, *Rediscovering Institutions: The Organizational Basis of Politics* (New York: Free Press, 1989).

[110]Ibid., 8.

Table 1.   Alternative Mechanisms of Europeanization

Mechanisms of Europeanization		
	Logic of Europeanization	
Principal actor initiating the process of Europeanization	Logic of consequences	Logic of appropriateness
European Union	Conditionality	Socialization
Ukraine	Externalization	Imitation

Source: Created by author.

Conditionality is perhaps the best known and studied mechanism of Europeanization and involves the direct impact of the European Union in a cost-benefit analysis.[111] Under the mechanization of conditionality, the European Union initiates the process of Europeanization using an incentives-based policy that rewards the Europeanizing state.[112] The most relevant rewards for the non-member state are different

---

[111]See, Hans Agné, "European Union Conditionality: Coercion or Voluntary Adaptation?" *Alternatives: Turkish Journal of International Relations* 8, no. 1 (Spring 1999), http://www. alternativesjournal.net (accessed March 16, 2012); Heather Grabbe, "European Union Conditionality and the *Acquis Communautaire,*" *International Political Science Review* 23, no. 3 (July 2002): 249-268.

[112]Ukraine is not a candidate for membership in the European Union, and so the term must not be construed to imply that Ukraine is in fact a candidate. If the European Union is driving the process of Europeanization in Ukraine, it must initially offer external incentives and rewards other than the prospect of membership within the European Union. An historical example here may be the European Commission's TACIS program. Between 1991 and 2006, TACIS provided foreign and technical assistance to members of the Common-wealth of Independent States (CIS) in their transition to democratic market-oriented economies. For example, TACIS promoted and financed nuclear safety projects, in particular The Nuclear Safety Co-operation Instrument, among the CIS, but did so without the offer of European Union membership.

types of agreements ranging from free trade areas and association agreements with provisions for obtaining financial support and technical assistance and accessing the single market, to full accession treaties. With respect to the Central and Eastern European countries of the 2004 Eastern enlargement, membership was conditional on candidate countries meeting the Copenhagen criteria and adopting the *acquis communautaire*.[113]

Related to conditionality is socialization; the European Union directly attempts to disseminate its beliefs and values by changing or altering preferences in other countries.[114] Conditionality and socialization are direct mechanisms initiated by the European Union to encourage non-member states to undertake the process of Europeanization. Unlike conditionality, however, socialization offers the non-member state few incentives or rewards from the European Union. Because of the absence of material incentives or rewards, socialization may be a more appropriate mechanism of Europeanization for non-European states which are less likely to seek membership in the European Union, but with which the European Union wants to encourage stronger ties. The North African countries of Morocco, Tunisia and Algeria--members of the European Neighbourhood Policy--may be appropriate countries for socialization. One of the

---

[113]The cumulative body of European Union laws, comprising the objectives, substantive rules, policies and, in particular, primary and secondary legislation and case law – all of which form part of the legal order of the European Union. This includes all the treaties, regulations and directives passed by the European institutions, as well as judgments laid down by the European Court of Justice. It comprises more than 80,000 pages of legislation.

[114]See, Jeffrey T. Checkel, "International Institutions and Socialization in Europe: Introduction and Framework," International Organization 59, no. 4 (Autumn 2005): 801-806.

advantages of socialization is that it aims to prevent the emergence of new dividing lines between the European Union and its non-European neighbours.

Externalization, by contrast, is a process of Europeanization in which non-member states assume the initiative and adapt domestic laws, policies and institutions to the standards of the European Union.[115] Similar to conditionality, externalization involves a cost-benefit analysis, but from the perspective of the non-member state. Attracted to potential rewards and incentives such as an association agreement and free trade area, a non-member state may initiate Europeanization efforts to encourage the European Union to open negotiations or extend financial support and technical assistance. In practical terms, conditionality and externalization may simply be two sides of the same coin.

Closely related to externalization is imitation, which serves as a mechanism for European integration, in which a non-member state seeks to mirror European Union policies, values and norms. The European Union serves as a model of governance, which other states emulate. Similar to the European Union-initiated mechanism of socialization, imitation best applies to non-European states which adopt European Union values and standards simply as a result of perceived appropriateness. There is no promise or reward offered by the European Union; instead a non-European state draws lessons from the European Union and amends its own domestic rules and policies. Externalization and

---

[115]See, Stefan Gänzle, "Externalizing EU Governance and the European Neighbourhood Policy: a Framework for Analysis," presentation prepared for "The EU as a Global Actor" Conference at Dalhousie University EU Centre of Excellence 5-6 May 2008, http://euce.dal.ca/Files/Ganzle.pdf (accessed March 16, 2012).

imitation are indirect mechanisms initiated by a non-member state, without the European

Union making any strong efforts.

The process of Europeanization occurs through the manipulation of incentives and

cost-benefit calculations in non-member states. In other words, coercion, external

incentives and bargaining about rewards are characteristic of conditionality and

externalization. The provision of material incentives by the European Union figures

prominently in these two approaches to Europeanization, especially conditionality which

is often seen as a strategy of reinforcement by reward.[116] In their various cases studies,

Schimmelfennig and Sedelmeier based their methodology on looking at certain areas of

European Union rules which the countries of Central and Eastern Europe would not have

adopted had it not been for a particular action or incentive offered by the European

Union.[117] In the past, external incentives have included technical and financial assistance

within such programs as the European Union's Poland and Hungary: Assistance for

Restructuring their Economies (PHARE) and the European Commission's Technical

Assistance to the Commonwealth of Independent States (TACIS) program.[118]

---

[116]Schimmelfennig and Sedelmeier, eds., *The Europeanization of Central and Eastern Europe*, 8.

[117]This was the case, for example, with the adoption of European Union air pollution policies in the Czech Republic. See, Liliana Andonova, "The Europeanization of Environmental Policy in Central and Eastern Europe," in Schimmelfennig and Sedelmeier, eds., *The Europeanization of Central and Eastern Europe*, 135-155.

[118]PHARE was redesigned to prepare states for accession to the European Union and was extended later to the other candidate states of Central and Eastern Europe. The European Union launched the TACIS program in 1991. It provided grant-financed technical assistance to 12 countries of Eastern Europe and Central Asia. The TACIS program has since been replaced for the countries of the European Neighbourhood Policy and Russia by the European Neighbourhood and Partnership Instrument.

The methodology for this research looks at the various bilateral agreements and annual progress reports issued by the European Commission and the Council of Europe and addresses the four mechanisms of Europeanization using criteria relevant to each of them. This methodology applies the same criteria to each of the three areas of this comparative case study: economic integration, energy cooperation, and judicial reform. This method facilitates comparison and ensures that the three areas are analyzed equally.

For the mechanism of conditionality, questions pertaining to whether the European Union has offered any incentive or reward to Ukraine to undertake the process of Europeanization are relevant. For example, has the European Union offered Ukraine any agreement or structured plan in exchange for Ukraine approximating its domestic economic and energy laws and its judiciary consistent with European Union standards and the *acquis communautaire*? Has the European Union offered Ukraine the promise of entering into an association agreement or a free trade area that would remove trade barriers? Conversely is the European Union withholding the signing of any agreement or promised reward of increased access to the single market as a consequence of Ukraine's failure to Europeanize? Has the European Union pledged financial support or technical assistance to assist Ukraine in modernizing its laws and institutions in an effort to attain standards consistent with those of the European Union? Has the European Union promised to assist Ukraine in securing membership in a European organization, such as the European Energy Community, in exchange for undertaking the process of Europeanization?

If the mechanism of conditionality is to describe Ukraine's efforts at Europeanizing its economic and energy policies, as well as it judicial institutions, one would expect to find the promise of bilateral agreements between the European Union and Ukraine and the pledge of financial support and technical assistance. Evidence suggesting Ukraine's Europeanization would be apparent from annual progress reports confirming that Ukraine is in fact approximating its laws and adopting concrete structural reforms. European Union bilateral agreements include provisions requiring the signatory state uphold European Union legal norms and values, such as respect for the rule of law and guarantees of a free and independent judiciary. Do the annual progress reports confirm or criticize Ukraine's efforts at judicial reform? Similarly, do the reports of the Council of Europe's Venice Commission approve of Ukraine's efforts to reform its judiciary and ensure its independence from political influence? These reports are relevant because the European Union may withhold signing an association agreement or entering into a free trade area if the Council of Europe's reports reflect negatively on Ukraine's efforts to reform its judiciary.

Similar criteria and questions are asked when assessing whether the mechanism of externalization is appropriate to describe Ukraine's efforts at Europeanization. Under the indirect mechanism of externalization, the European Union does not actively promote its model or rules of governance beyond its own borders. Nonetheless, the impact of its 27-member internal market, and the fact that the European Union is the world's largest donor of foreign assistance, cannot be ignored--least of all by a neighbouring state like Ukraine which relies on the European Union for one-third of its external trade. Consequently, a non-member European country may voluntarily adopt and follow European Union rules because to ignore or violate them could negatively impact their own domestic economic or political arrangement. A country whose economy is strongly interconnected with that of the European Union will make its own internal rules compatible with those of the European Union.

Externalization as a mechanism for driving Europeanization in Ukraine is relevant insofar as Ukraine needs or desires access to Europe's internal market. Is Europeanization by externalization also at work within Ukraine? Instead of the external incentives and rewards initiated by the European Union, the source material might indicate whether Ukraine is initiating the process of Europeanization by adopting domestic reforms aimed at seeking increased integration with the European Union. For example, is Ukraine engaging the European Union, offering to Europeanize its economic, energy and judicial sectors, in return for rewards of increased access to the single market, the signing of an association agreement, or a free trade area? Is there evidence that Ukraine is modernizing its energy sector because of the twofold benefit of obtaining further integration with the European Energy Community while decreasing its dependence on Russia's natural energy resources? Is Ukraine not only receptive to whatever incentives may be offered by the European Union, but actually leading the process of Europeanization by exercising its initiative in matters of economic integration and energy cooperation? In matters of judicial reform, is Ukraine soliciting the Council of Europe's Venice Commission for advice on amending its laws pertaining to its judiciary?

The direct, European Union-driven, mechanism of socialization and the indirect mechanism of imitation, represent a "logic of appropriateness" model of Europeanization and are not based on external incentives or rewards.[119] Socialization and imitation are

---

[119]An example of this is the adoption of European Union air emission standards by Poland and Czechoslovakia (later the Czech Republic) in the early 1990s, several

described by Schimmelfennig as social learning models of Europeanization in which a non-member state identifies with the European Union.[120] A state adopts European Union rules because it "judges them as effective remedies to inherently *domestic* needs and policy challenges, rather than out of considerations about the incentives that the European Union might offer for rule adoption."[121] Emphasis is placed on the legitimacy of rules and appropriateness of behavior, and not so much on the bargaining about conditions and rewards. Criteria relevant to assessing these models include whether Ukraine simply identifies with the European Union, adapting its laws and policies consistent with the European Union, but without seeking any reward or incentive for Europeanizing. Is Ukraine Europeanizing its economic, energy and judicial sectors independent of any perceived benefit of an association agreement or the promise of financial support or technical assistance? Similar questions may be posed, but the findings may disclose that socialization and imitation would appear to be insufficient mechanisms defining Ukraine's approach to Europeanization. After all, Ukraine is a European state that has consistently defended its European identity; it aspires to further integration with the European Union and perhaps even eventual membership. In 2010, Ukraine was the European Union's 23rd largest trading partner and 19th largest export market. The European Union is Ukraine's second largest trading partner, with 25.3 percent of the total

---

years before either country became a formal candidate for European Union membership. See, Liliana Andonova, "The Europeanization of Environmental Policy in Central and Eastern Europe," in Schimmelfennig and Sedelmeier, eds., *The Europeanization of Central and Eastern Europe*, 135-155.

[120]Schimmelfennig and Sedelmeier, eds., *The Europeanization of Central and Eastern Europe*, 9.

[121]Ibid., 10. Emphasis in original.

50

exports and 31.4 percent of imports in 2010.[122] The interconnectedness of Ukraine and the European Union is such that the mechanisms of socialization and imitation may simply underestimate the relevance of Ukraine's Europeanization.

This comparative case study looks explicitly at the areas of economic integration, energy cooperation, and judicial reform consisting in the adaptation of Ukrainian law consistent with the *acquis communautaire*. These three areas were chosen in part to reflect the general policy areas addressed in the Copenhagen Criteria: stability of legislative institutions, existence of a functioning market economy, and adherence to political, economic and monetary union. Arguably energy cooperation may not be an ideal match in which to assess adherence to political, economic and monetary union. Nonetheless, Ukraine has signed onto a number of energy treaties and agreements with the European Union;[123] Ukraine's adherence to their terms and requirements, which include approximation of Ukrainian law to that of the European Union energy *acquis*, may be a valuable indicator of whether Ukraine is undertaking the process of Europeanization.

---

[122]European Union External Action Service, Delegation of the European Union to Ukraine, EU-Ukraine bilateral trade, http://eeas.europa.eu/delegations/ukraine/eu_ ukraine/trade_relation/bilateral_trade/index_en.htm (accessed March 15, 2012).

[123]See, Energy Charter Treaty, European Energy Community, and Agreement between the European Atomic Energy Community and the Cabinet of Ministers of Ukraine for Co-operation in the Peaceful Uses of Nuclear Energy the Ukraine and European Commission Agreement for Nuclear Energy Cooperation. See also, Memorandum of Understanding on Co-operation in the Field of Energy between the European Union and Ukraine, December 1, 2005, http://ec.europa.eu/dgs/energy_ transport/transport/international/bilateral/ukraine/doc/mou_en_final_en.pdf (accessed March 16, 2012).

The strength of relying on Schimmelfennig's and Sedelmeier's four mechanisms of Europeanization is that they have proven valid for assessing the Europeanization efforts of the countries of Central and Eastern Europe. Relying on these four mechanisms and applying the methodology outlined in this chapter may lead to a valid assessment of whether Ukraine is Europeanizing in the areas of economic integration, energy cooperation and judicial reform. Any broad or sweeping conclusions about Ukraine's efforts to Europeanize must be qualified, however, since the four mechanisms and the application of the methodology are limited to three areas: economics, energy, and judicial reform. Many other areas, including social and regional policy, agriculture, environmental policy, and consumer and health protection need to be similarly examined to determine the true extent of Europeanization in Ukraine. In addition, it must be emphasized that Schimmelfennig's and Sedelmeier's case studies looked exclusively at the Central and Eastern European countries which at the time were officially recognized candidate states for European Union membership. The promised reward of membership and its perceived benefits, for example, access to the internal market, relaxation of visa requirements, and the absence of trade barriers, served as considerable incentives for the countries of Central and Eastern Europe to Europeanize beginning in the mid-to-late 1990s. The case of Ukraine is different; Ukraine is not (yet) a candidate for European Union membership.

CHAPTER 4

DATA FINDINGS AND ANALYSIS

This chapter addresses the findings of the research involving the areas of

Ukraine's economic integration, cooperation in energy policy, and judicial reform using

the methodological approach outlined in chapter 3 to determine whether Ukraine is

undergoing the process of Europeanization. If Ukraine is in the process of adopting

European Union rules in these areas, this research will then determine who initiated the

drive to Europeanize: Ukraine or the European Union. The findings will then address

which of the four mechanisms of Europeanization identified by Schimmelfennig and

Sedelmeier are most appropriate to characterize the logic of Ukraine's rule adoption:

conditionality, externalization, socialization or imitation? This part of the research and

findings leads to a conclusion addressing Ukraine's motivation to undergo the process of

Europeanization and whether its efforts to Europeanize follow a "logic of consequences"

or a "logic of appropriateness" model.

Recalling his 1998 study, James Sherr criticized Ukraine's efforts at seeking

increased integration with the European Union as having amounted to little more than

joining international organizations and political clubs without undertaking concrete

structural changes that would have brought Ukraine closer to European Union norms and

values.[124] Six years later, Kataryna Wolczuk characterized Ukraine's policy towards the

European Union as one of integration without Europeanization. She found that simply

seeking integration through foreign policy instruments, such as the 1998 Partnership and

---

[124]Sherr, *Ukraine's New Time of Troubles*, 11.

Cooperation Agreement, had not actually fostered domestic and institutional reforms within Ukraine.[125] The findings and analysis presented in this chapter attempt to determine whether their criticisms remain valid or whether Ukraine has progressed in its efforts to Europeanize, thus securing a future of increased integration with Europe.

Economic Integration: the Joint European Union-Ukraine Action Plan and the European Union-Ukraine Association Agenda

Using Schimmelfennig's and Sedelmeier's four mechanisms of Europeanization and the methodology outlined in chapter 3, this section presents evidence that suggests Ukraine is achieving increased economic integration with the European Union. Bilateral agreements and annual progress reports issued by the European Union indicate that Ukraine has been adopting economic measures aimed at approaching European Union standards. The analysis that follows suggests that the push to Europeanize is best characterized as a joint effort between the European Union and Ukraine. The analysis addresses each of the four mechanisms using the criteria and questions outlined in chapter 3. The evidence suggests that the mechanisms of conditionality and externalization appropriately describe Ukraine's path to Europeanize and that its efforts follow a "logic of consequences" approach. The analysis also poses questions to the alternative methods of Europeanization: socialization and imitation. Criteria relevant to assessing these models include whether Ukraine has Europeanized its economic laws and policies, regardless of whether the European Union offered any reward or incentive to do so. Because of the significant bilateral agreements between the European Union and Ukraine and the incentives contained in their provisions, these two lesson drawing

---

[125]Wolczuk, "Integration without Europeanisation," 21-22.

models of Europeanization prove less apt to describe Ukraine's efforts. Evidence suggesting this is the fact that Ukraine's leadership has consistently expressed a desire for increased European integration, with many Ukrainians advocating for full membership, and that the European Union continues to view Ukraine as a priority partner in its Eastern Partnership program.

Since Wolzcuk's study, the European Union has implemented a number of programs and foreign policy initiatives designed to foster increased cooperation with its non-member neighbours. In 2004, the European Union developed the European Neighbourhood Policy in an effort to avoid the emergence of new dividing lines between the enlarged European Union and its neighbours in Eastern Europe, the South Caucasus and the South shore of the Mediterranean, and to strengthen "the prosperity, stability, and security of all."[126] Central to the European Neighbourhood Policy are bilateral Action Plans between the European Union and each partner state.[127] An Action Plan is a political document which sets out an agenda of political and economic reforms with short and medium-term priorities of three to five years. Implementation of the European Neighbourhood Policy is jointly promoted and monitored through the committees and sub-committees established within each Action Plan. In addition, the European Commission publishes annual European Neighbourhood Policy Progress Reports.[128]

---

[126]See European Commission, European Neighbourhood Policy, http://ec.europa. eu/world/enp/index_en.htm (accessed March 20, 2012).

[127]Ibid. Twelve of the 16 partner countries have already adopted a European Neighbourhood Policy Action Plan. Algeria, Belarus, Libya and Syria have not.

[128]The most recent progress report on Ukraine covers the period through 2010. See, European Commission, *Joint Staff Working Paper: Implementation of the European Neighbourhood Policy in 2010*, May 25, 2011 SEC(2011) 646, COM(2011) 303,

There are no legal sanctions for failure to implement commitments contained in an Action Plan. In such situations, the consequences would be political, impacting the overall relationship with the partner country, as well as financial, affecting the assistance provided in support of a particular policy area.[129] The European Union and Ukraine jointly adopted an Action Plan on February 21, 2005.[130] According to the European Commission, the European Neighbourhood Policy "provides an excellent basis for strengthening" the European Union's relationship with Ukraine "by encouraging reform and by offering a substantial degree of economic integration as well as deeper political cooperation."[131] Most importantly, the Joint European Union-Ukraine Action Plan became the political instrument for steering European Union-Ukraine relations in all areas of cooperation.

Initially designed to cover a period of three years, the Joint European Union-Ukraine Action Plan signaled "an important new step" in the strategic partnership between the European Union and Ukraine and confirmed the latter's European

---

http://ec.europa.eu/world/enp/pdf/progress2011/sec_11_646_en.pdf (accessed March 20, 2012). For 2005–2009 progress reports see, http://ec.europa.eu/world/enp/documents_en.htm (accessed March 20, 2012).

[129]Ibid.

[130]For the full 43-page text of the *Joint European Union – Ukraine Action Plan*, see, http://ec.europa.eu/world/enp/pdf/action_plans/ukraine_enp_ap_final_en.pdf (accessed March 20, 2012). Preceding the Action Plan was a 24-page *European Neighbourhood Policy Country Report: Ukraine,* published in May 2004.

[131]European Commission, European Neighbourhood Policy, "The Policy: Frequently Asked Questions," http://ec.europa.eu/world/enp/faq_en.htm (accessed March 20, 2012).

aspirations.[132] There is no explicit reference to Europeanization in the text of the Action Plan; nonetheless, implementation of the Action Plan was designed to "significantly advance the approximation of Ukrainian legislation, norms and standards to those of the European Union" and to "build solid foundations for further economic integration, including through joint efforts towards a European Union-Ukraine Free Trade Area."[133] The Action Plan is divided into a number of chapters: political dialogue and reform, economic and social reform and development, trade, market and regulatory reform, cooperation in justice and home affairs, transport, energy, information society and environment, and people-to-people contacts.[134]

Participation in the European Neighbourhood Policy and implementation of the Action Plan have been viewed by the European Union as affording Ukraine the "opportunity for convergence of economic legislation, the opening of economies to each other, and the continued reduction of trade barriers."[135] In addition, the Action Plan outlines a comprehensive set of priorities intended to move beyond the scope of the 1998 Partnership and Cooperation Agreement. Included among these "Priorities for Action" is the "[g]radual approximation of Ukrainian legislation, norms and standards with those of the European Union" aimed at "further reinforcing administrative and judicial capacity."[136] The 43-page document contains a number of references to economic

---

[132]*Joint European Union-Ukraine Action Plan*, February 21, 2005, 1.

[133]Ibid.

[134]Ibid.

[135]Ibid., 2.

[136]Ibid., 4.

integration and cooperation encouraging what may be characterized as Ukraine's efforts to Europeanize its economic laws and policies and represents a significant achievement by the European Union to strengthen its relations with Ukraine.

While silent on the actual wording of Europeanization, the Action Plan nonetheless clearly encouraged Ukraine to commit itself to the process of Europeanization by approximating its domestic economic legislation to that of the European Union. This raises the obvious question: How well did Ukraine implement the 2005 Action Plan by beginning an approximation of its economic legislation with that of the European Union? In other words, did Ukraine begin the process of Europeanization within its domestic economic legislation? The answer is to be found in European Neighbourhood Policy Progress Reports on Ukraine published annually by the European Commission with the first appearing in December 2006.[137]

The 2006 Progress Report summarized evaluations made in November 2005 and March 2006 and addressed the overall progress of Ukraine's implementation of the Action Plan. The Report found that despite introducing "a wide range of legislative reforms" Ukraine's progress in implementing the Action Plan was "being hindered by endemic corruption, which is the main challenge to the development and economic

---

[137]European Commission, *European Neighbourhood Policy Progress Report, Ukraine*, Staff Working Document Accompanying the Communication from the Commission to the Council and the European Parliament on Strengthening the European Neighbourhood Policy, COM(2006) 726 final, 4 December 2006, SEC(2006) 1505/2, http://ec.europa.eu/world/enp/pdf/sec06_1505-2_en.pdf (accessed March 20, 2012). An earlier *Country Report for Ukraine* published in May 2004, presented a general review of the political and economic situation in Ukraine. See, http://ec.europa.eu/world/enp/pdf/country/ukraine_enp_country_report_2004_en.pdf (accessed March 20, 2012).

growth of Ukraine, and by the lack of a truly independent judiciary."[138] As of December 2006, Ukraine lacked "a clear-cut economic policy" and the authors of the Report expressed "particular concerns about loose monetary and fiscal policies."[139] The Report identified the need for Ukraine to adopt "significant further steps . . . to improve the business climate, including administrative and legislative reform, improving tax regulation and administration and further fighting corruption."[140]

All was not negative, however. On the free movement of goods and technical regulations, Ukraine "confirmed its commitment to negotiate an Agreement of Conformity Assessment and Acceptance of Industrial Products" and Ukraine adopted laws on "standards, technical regulations and conformity assessment procedures and on consumer protection" in 2006.[141] The 2006 Progress Report acknowledged Ukraine's efforts to improve its business community by first eliminating barriers to the establishment of companies adopted in a September 2005 law on licensing. This law simplified licensing legislation and sharply reduced the time and number of permissions required to start a business. The same year, Ukraine adopted a new law protecting economic competition. There was, however, less progress in the area of company law and on developing a framework of corporate governance and on modernizing Ukraine's system of accounting.[142] The Progress Report concluded by summarizing the financial

---

[138]Ibid., 2.

[139]Ibid.

[140]Ibid., 3.

[141]Ibid., 10.

[142]Ibid., 10.

assistance provided to Ukraine by the European Union, noting that it had "increased substantially in recent years from €50 million in 2003 to €100 million in 2006" and that financial allocation would increase further along with "the strategic, policy-driven character of . . . assistance programmes to Ukraine."[143]

Following the expiration of the initial Action Plan, Ukraine and the European Union adopted a "Revised European Union-Ukraine Action Plan on Freedom, Security and Justice Challenges and Strategic Aims" on June 18, 2007.[144] The European Commission issued annual progress reports on the implementation of the European Neighbourhood Policy in Ukraine for 2007 and 2008.[145] The Progress Report for 2007 noted that Ukraine "continued to make progress in most areas, although the pace of progress stalled somewhat compared to the previous years, in particular as regards economic and structural reforms . . . due to the political instability which characterised most of 2007."[146] The 2007 Progress Report noted that there had been no progress regarding "the establishment of a modern company law," "no progress in the area of

---

[143]Ibid., 17.

[144]European Commission, *Revised European Union-Ukraine Action Plan on Freedom, Security and Justice Challenges and Strategic Aims*, June 18, 2007, http://ec. europa.eu/world/enp/pdf/action_plans/ukraine_enp_ap_jls-rev_en.pdf (accessed March 20, 2012).

[145]For the 2007 and 2008 Progress Reports, see, European Commission, *Implementation of the European Neighbourhood Policy in 2007 Progress Report Ukraine*, Staff Working Document Accompanying the Communication from the Commission to the Council and the European Parliament, COM(2008) 164, 3 April 2008, SEC(2008) 402; European Commission, *Implementation of the European Neighbourhood Policy in 2008 Progress Report Ukraine*, Staff Working Document Accompanying the Communication from the Commission to the Council and the European Parliament, COM(2009) 188, 23 April 2009, SEC(2009) 515/2.

[146]European Commission, *2007 Progress Report Ukraine*, 2.

freedom of capital movements," "no significant progress in the area of taxation," and "no progress with regard to the transparency and independence of the competition agency, the Anti-Monopoly Committee of Ukraine."[147] Similarly, the 2008 Progress Report reported little progress in the area of economic reform and approximation of Ukraine's economic laws to that of the European Union. The 2008 Progress Report noted that although "Ukraine made progress in several areas covered by the Joint European Union-Ukraine Action Plan in the course of 2008 and continued to come closer to the European Union through negotiations on an Association Agreement . . . the continuing political instability was not conducive to reform."[148]

The European Commission continued to monitor progress in implementation of the Action Plan until 2009, when it was replaced by the European Union-Ukraine Association Agenda adopted by the European Union-Ukraine Cooperation Council on November 23, 2009, and which entered into force the following day.[149] This Association Agenda served as an interim agreement for the subsequent rounds of negotiations that

---

[147]Ibid., 10-11.

[148]European Commission, *2008 Progress Report Ukraine*, 2.

[149]European Commission, *European Union-Ukraine Association Agenda to prepare and facilitate the implementation of the Association Agreement*, 1, http://www. eeas.europa.eu/ukraine/docs/2010_ eu_ukraine_association_agenda_en.pdf (accessed March 15, 2012). Earlier, the European Union-Ukraine Cooperation Council endorsed the Association Agenda on June 16, 2009. Plans for negotiating a joint European Union-Ukraine Association Agreement were introduced at the European Union-Ukraine Summit held in Paris, September 9, 2008. See, Council of the European Union, *EU-Ukraine Summit, Paris, 9 September 2008,* 12812/08 (Presse 247), http://www.consilium.europa. eu/uedocs/cms_data/docs/pressdata/en/er/102633.pdf (accessed March 20, 2012). The launch of negotiations followed the finalization of Ukraine's accession to the World Trade Organization on February 5, 2008, with Ukraine formally becoming a member on May 16, 2008, a prerequisite for the start of free trade negotiations.

have since led to the drafting of a new Association Agreement designed to "facilitate the deepening of relations in all areas and strengthen political association and economic integration through reciprocal rights and obligations."[150] The European Union and Ukraine acknowledged that "gradual convergence of Ukraine with the European Union in the political, economic and legal areas would contribute to further progress" in their bi-lateral relations.[151] In terms of economic integration, the European Union agreed "to support Ukraine in establishing a fully functioning market economy and gradually approximating its policies to the policies of the Community in accordance with the guiding principles of macroeconomic stability, sound public finances, a robust financial system and sustainable balance of payments."[152]

The same year also marked the start of the Eastern Partnership program. The European Union, following the recommendation of Poland and Sweden, initiated the Eastern Partnership in May 2009, in part to "promote democracy and good governance, strengthen energy security" and "support economic and social development and offer additional funding for projects to reduce socio-economic imbalances and increase stability" within the six partner countries that comprise the Eastern Partnership.[153] Eastern Partnership "offers its Eastern partners concrete, far-reaching support for democratic and market-oriented reforms," thus contributing to their political and

---

[150]Ibid., 2.

[151]Ibid.

[152]Ibid., 15.

[153]See, European Union External Action Service, Eastern Partnership, http://eeas. europa.eu/ eastern/index_en.htm (accessed March 16, 2012).

economic stability.[154] This does not assume, however, that Eastern Partnership is the means by which the European Union will assist Ukraine in undergoing the process of Europeanization. At the time Eastern Partnership was initiated in May 2009, the Czech Republic held the Presidency of the Council of the European Union.[155] In connection with the Russian-Ukrainian gas crisis at the outset of 2009, Czech authorities voiced confidence in the Eastern Partnership and the urgent necessity of raising energy security. Alluding to Ukraine's significant role in the Eastern Partnership, Czech authorities declared that it would "be an instrument that will encourage Ukraine to tidy up its intransparent economic structures, especially in the energy field, and to strengthen market mechanisms." Further, the Eastern Partnership would bring Eastern neighbourhood countries like Ukraine "closer to European Union standards."[156]

Shortly after adopting the Association Agenda, the European Commission issued a List of the European Union-Ukraine Association Agenda priorities for 2010.[157] A Joint Committee at Senior Official's Level of European Union-Ukraine Association Agenda agreed to this list on January 26, 2010, which set forth priorities to be accomplished in order to conclude an Association Agreement. Implementing strategic plans for state tax

---

[154]European Union External Action Service, Press Release, Eastern Partnership MEMO/09/217, May 5, 2009, http:// europa.eu/rapid/pressReleasesAction.do?reference= MEMO/ 09/217&format=HTML &aged= &language=EN&guiLanguage=en (accessed March 16, 2012).

[155]The Czech Republic held the presidency of the European Union Council from January 1 until June 30, 2009. See, http://www.eu2009.cz/en/ (accessed March 20, 2012).

[156]Wojna and Gniazdowski, eds., *Eastern Partnership: the Opening Report*, 22.

[157]European Commission, *List of the European Union-Ukraine Association Agenda priorities for 2010*, http://www.eeas.europa.eu/ukraine/docs/2010_association_ agenda_priorities_en.pdf (accessed March 20, 2012).

administration, improving the functioning of company law, corporate governance, accounting and auditing, and implementing a regulatory framework for financial markets are just a few of the 78 priorities enumerated in the 10-page document. The following summer a joint committee of European Union and Ukrainian officials issued a Joint Report on the progress of implementing the Association Agenda.[158] The report noted the following progress: "For its part the Ukrainian Government adopted a Resolution setting out priority measures for 2010 to support the process of political association and economic integration with the European Union as well as a comprehensive Programme of Economic Reforms announced by the President of Ukraine on 2nd June [2010]."[159]

Similar to the Joint European Union-Ukraine Action Plan, the European Commission published annual progress reports assessing the European Union-Ukraine Association Agenda. The 3rd Joint Progress Report, issued November 26, 2009, cited remarkable progress in the five preceding rounds of negotiations.

A strong joint commitment to advance has allowed all 31 chapters on economic and sector cooperation to be provisionally closed, promising the implementation

---

[158]Joint Report Regarding Progress in Implementation of the Joint Committee at Senior Official Level of the EU-Ukraine Association Agenda to the EU-Ukraine Co-operation Council, Brussels/Kyiv, June 2010, http://www.eeas.europa.eu/ukraine/docs/ 2010_eu-ukraine_joint_ report_association_agenda_en.pdf (accessed March 20, 2012).

[159]Ibid., 2. Ukraine adopted Resolution 1073 of 19 May 2010, Priority Measures to integrate Ukraine into the European Union for 2010. The Joint Committee of the Association Agenda at Senior Official's level endorsed a subsequent updated version of the European Union-Ukraine Association Agenda, as well as List of the European Union-Ukraine Association Agenda Priorities for 2011, on May 20, 2011. See, European Commission, European Union-Ukraine Association Agenda to Prepare and Facilitate the Implementation of the Association Agreement, http://www.eeas.europa.eu/ukraine/docs/ 2011_eu-ukraine_association_agenda_update_en.pdf (accessed March 20, 2012); European Commission, List of the European Union-Ukraine Association Agenda Priorities for 2011, http://www.eeas.europa.eu/ukraine/docs/2011_12_eu_ukraine_ priorities_en.pdf (accessed March 20, 2012).

by Ukraine of critical European Union laws and standards in areas as diverse as environment, public health, agriculture and transport.[160]

The 2009 Progress Report highlighted specific progress in economic integration and Ukraine's implementation of European Union laws and standards:

> In the group on Economic and Sector Cooperation, negotiations on all 31 areas have been finalised, opening the way for a comprehensive implementation by Ukraine of core European Union laws and standards which will impact on the context in which economic activities will be conducted, and on the lives of citizens. These include agriculture and rural development; audio-visual policy; civil society cooperation; company law; consumer protection; cross-border and regional cooperation; culture; the Danube river; education, training, and youth; financial cooperation including anti-fraud provisions; energy cooperation; environment; financial services; fisheries and maritime development; health policy; industrial and enterprise policy; information society; macro-economic cooperation; management of public finances; mining and metals; participationin Community agencies and programmes; research and technological development; social cooperation; space; sports; statistics; taxation; tourism; and transport.[161]

Following agreement that Ukraine would accede to the World Trade Organization (formal accession occurred on May 16, 2008), European Union Commissioner Peter Mandelson and Ukrainian President Viktor Yushchenko launched negotiations on a Deep and Comprehensive Free Trade Area (DCFTA), as a core element of the Association Agreement, on February 18, 2008. As the words deep and comprehensive imply, a DCFTA is "an ambitious undertaking providing access to most of the European Union's internal market."[162] It covers a wide range of trade-related matters ("comprehensive")

---

[160]European Commission, *3rd Joint Progress Report, Negotiations on the European Union-Ukraine Association Agreement*, Brussels/Kyiv, November 26, 2009, 1, http://www.eeas.europa.eu/ukraine/docs/assoc_agreement_3rd_joint_progress_ report.pdf (accessed March 20, 2012).

[161]Ibid., 2.

[162]Per Magnus Wijkman, "Fostering Deep and Comprehensive Free Trade Agreements for the Eastern Partners," *Eastern Partnership Review* no. 8 (Tallinn:

and aims at eliminating obstacles to trade through processes of regulatory approximation and partially opening the European Union's internal market to Ukraine ("deep"). A DCFTA will achieve much more than a simple free trade agreement; it would simplify trade contacts between the European Union and Ukraine, improve Ukraine's business climate and positively influence the economic situation in the country. Moreover, Ukrainian laws and standards would become compatible with those of the European Union in trade and trade-related areas.[163]

European Union economic and social policy is summed up under the four freedoms--free movement of goods, capital, services and persons. A DCFTA grants three of the four freedoms--free movement of substantially all goods, many services and capital--and aims at a high level of integration.[164] Among the anticipated benefits for Ukraine is a better domestic investment climate. The DCFTA would spur changes in national legislation and an adjustment to European Union standards and regulations, resulting in greater transparency and a set of rules familiar to foreign investors. A 4th Joint Progress Report issued November 8, 2010, highlights significant accomplishments during the negotiations between the European Union and Ukraine on the establishment of a DCFTA. The Report notes that the establishment of a DCFTA "will lead to ever deeper integration of Ukraine into the European Union internal market, in parallel with the

---

Estonian Center of Eastern Partnership, December 2011), http://www.eceap.eu/ (accessed March 20, 2012).

[163]Karl De Gucht, "A trade deal for growth," Diplomatic Academy, Kyiv, October 28, 2010, http://trade.ec.europa.eu/doclib/docs/2010/october/tradoc_146837.pdf (accessed March 20, 2012).

[164]Ibid.

implementation of relevant elements of the *acquis*. Ukraine reiterated its continuing

attachment to this ultimate goal through gradual extension of the four freedoms to

Ukraine."[165]

On October 20, 2011, following the conclusion of the 19th round of negotiations,

Ukraine's Vice Prime Minister Andriy Klyuyev and the European Commissioner for

Trade, Karel De Gucht, reached agreement on all elements of the DCFTA. At his speech

before the European Parliament the following day, Commissioner De Gucht called upon

Ukraine's leadership "to create the political conditions wherein this deal can

materialize."[166] Conclusion of negotiations on the DCFTA between the European Union

and Ukraine is a good sign for the further integration of Ukraine and promises to be a

significant milestone supporting Ukraine's efforts to Europeanize.[167]

Significantly, the DCFTA is to be an integral part of a European Union-Ukraine

Association Agreement, which is to be the successor agreement to the Partnership and

Cooperation Agreement. At the 20th round of negotiations held on October 26, the

European Union and Ukraine concluded the political points of the Association

Agreement and there had been hope to sign the DCFTA and Association Agreement by

---

[165]European Commission, *4th Joint Progress Report, Negotiations on the European Union-Ukraine Association Agreement*, Brussels/Kyiv, November 8, 2010, http://www.eeas.europa.eu/ukraine/docs/joint_progress_report4_association_en.pdf (accessed March 20, 2012).

[166]See Commissioner Karel De Gucht's speech in the European Parliament October 20, 2011, http://www.eeas.europa.eu/delegations/ukraine/press_corner/all_ news/news/2011/2011_10_ 21_03_en.htm (accessed March 20, 2012).

[167]See, Marek Dabrowski and Svitlana Taran, *The Free Trade Agreement Between the EU and Ukraine: Conceptual Background, Economic Context and Potential Impact*, Brussels: European Parliament, Directorate-General for External Policies, October 2011, http://www.europarl.europa.eu (accessed March 20, 2012).

the end of 2011. Implementation of the Association Agreement with the European Union

is seen as an opportunity for Ukraine to improve its democratic institutions and promote

the rule of law. The signing of the deal, however, has been called into question following

the October 11, 2011 sentencing of former Prime Minister Yulia Tymoshenko to seven

years in prison for exceeding her authority in signing a 2009 gas deal with Russia. The

European Union strongly criticized the jailing of Tymoshenko, calling the decision to

imprison her politically motivated. European Council President Herman Van Rompuy

criticized the trial and conviction stating that "[t]he perceived deterioration of the quality

of democracy and rule of law in Ukraine has a direct impact in our Member-States, in our

public at large, and in the European Parliament."[168] Ukrainian President Viktor

Yanukovych responded to the criticism by simply confirming that "the European Union

remarks [would] not be ignored."[169] President Yanukovych was to have met with Van

Rompuy and José Manuel Barroso, the President of the European Commission, in

October to prepare the ground for the signing of Ukraine's Association Agreement at a

---

[168]"Ukraine, EU conclude association talks amid 'difficult atmosphere'," RIA Novosti, December 19, 2011, http://en.rian.ru/world/20111219/170374785.html (accessed March 20, 2012). See also, European Council, "Remarks of President Herman Van Rompuy, following the 15th EU-Ukraine Summit," Kyiv, December 19, 2011 (EUCO 166/11) (PRESSE 511): "Today, we publicly announce that negotiations on the Association Agreement have been finalized . . . We want to take steps to sign and ratify the Association Agreement as soon as we can, but this will depend on political circumstances . . . a number of recent domestic developments in Ukraine have led to a difficult atmosphere between the European Union and Ukraine."

[169]Ibid. Tymoshenko lost her appeal against her seven year prison sentence on December 23, 2011, following the decision made by the Kyiv Court of Appeals, which let stand the sentence imposed on Tymoshenko by the Kyiv Pechersky District Court. See, "Tymoshenko Sentence in Gas Supply Case Takes Legal Force," Kyiv Post, December 23, 2011, http://www.kyivpost.com/news/ (accessed March 20, 2012). Tymoshenko intends to lodge a complaint against the verdict at the European Court of Human Rights.

summit in December, but a spokeswoman for the European Commission has since remarked that the meeting would take place at a later date when conditions became "more conducive to progress in relations" and that much depends on "whether Ukraine respects the rule of law and the independence of the judiciary."[170] The European Commission postponed signing the Association Agreement on December 19, 2011. According to a European Commission spokeswoman, the European Union's unease was not only about Tymoshenko's fate but included a concern for the "a broader concept of fundamental values" within Ukraine.[171] Tymoshenko's trial and conviction highlights not so much European Union sympathy for her case, but rather Yanukovych's abuse of a core value of the European Union, the rule of law.[172]

Despite the apparent stalemate in the signing of the Association Agreement, it is clear that Ukraine has undertaken significant measures aimed at furthering its economic integration with the European Union. Beginning with the Joint European Union-Ukraine Action Plan of 2005, and continuing with the European Union-Ukraine Association Agenda of 2009 and the twenty successful rounds of negotiations leading to the finalization of a European Union-Ukraine Association Agreement in October 2011, the

---

[170]Toby Vogel, "EU Cancels Yanukovych Meeting," Europeanvoice.com, October 18, 2011, http://www.europeanvoice.com/article/2011/october/eu-cancels-yanukovych-meeting/72325.aspx (accessed March 20, 2012). See also, Interfax-Ukraine, "Kyiv's performance in sphere of rule of law to be crucial for subsequent implementation of association agreement," December 19, 2011, http://www.interfax.com.ua/eng/main/89367/ (accessed March 20, 2012).

[171]Vogel, "EU Cancels Yanukovych meeting."

[172]"Yulia Tymoshenko's Trials," *The Economist,* October 15, 2011. Commenting on Tymoshenko's fate, Carl Bildt, Sweden's foreign minister, remarked "of course, few saints grace Ukrainian politics . . . but whether saint or sinner, everyone deserves a fair hearing, not a show trial."

European Union and Ukraine have succeeded in advancing Ukraine's efforts at Europeanization. The European Union may have initiated the process, particularly through its European Neighbourhood Policy, but Ukraine must be seen as an equal partner, cooperating with the European Union.

Initially, the annual progress reports of the Joint European Union-Ukraine Action Plan disclosed little progress in Ukraine's efforts to Europeanize its economic laws and policies. With the Association Agenda of 2009, however, matters improved significantly; the progress reports provide convincing evidence of Ukraine's achievements in approximating its economic laws to those of the European Union. Despite remaining silent on the promise of European Union membership, the Joint European Union-Ukraine Action Plan and the Association Agenda offered Ukraine significant incentives to Europeanize in the form of financial and technical assistance to adopt domestic reforms and strengthen its political and economic integration with the European Union. Arguably, the promise of an Association Agreement and a DCFTA with the European Union proved suitable rewards spurring Ukraine's Europeanization efforts.

The findings and analysis based on the annual progress reports of the Joint European Union-Ukraine Action Plan and the successful rounds of negotiations that have since led to the drafting of an Association Agreement and the DCFTA suggest that the European Union initiated efforts to encourage the Europeanization of Ukraine. It is also evident that Ukraine has been a willing partner during the negotiations. Despite its silence on the promise of European Union membership, the 2005 Action Plan and the 2009 Association Agenda offered Ukraine significant financial support and technical assistance to adopt domestic reforms and strengthen political and economic integration with the

European Union.[173] The mechanism of conditionality seems most appropriate to describe

the European Union's efforts in advancing Ukraine's increased integration with Europe.

Conditionality must be qualified, however, since it rests not so much on the promise of

membership, but rather largely on the technical and financial assistance offered Ukraine

and the benefits to be gained from entering into an Association Agreement and

implementing the DCFTA. In addition, credit must be given to Ukraine, for as has been

noted throughout the various progress reports, Ukraine succeeded to a large extent in

achieving structural reforms, particularly within its domestic economic legislation, and

adopting European Union laws and policies. Ukraine's efforts may best be characterized

under the mechanism of externalization, adapting its domestic laws, policies and

institutions to the standards of the European Union. Using Schimmelfennig's and

Sedelmeier's logic of Europeanization model, one finds that the "logic of consequences"

is most appropriate to describe Ukraine's Europeanization efforts here. The signing of the

Association Agreement and implementation of the DCFTA may be an open question

because of the present controversy surrounding the trial and conviction of Yulia

Tymoshenko, but the benefits Ukraine stands to gain such as the elimination of trade

obstacles and the partial opening of the European Union's internal market are

considerable.

---

[173]Ibid., 35. "In the case of the European Community . . . support is to be provided in the context of the overall priorities for assistance in favour of Ukraine, as part of the overall funding available for Ukraine and in full respect of the relevant implementation rules and procedures of European Community external assistance."

Energy Cooperation: the Memorandum of Understanding on Co-operation
in the Field of Energy between the European Union and Ukraine

Similar to the findings of Ukraine's economic integration, this section identifies

Ukraine's successful efforts at Europeanizing its energy sector. Bilateral agreements on

energy cooperation and the peaceful uses of nuclear energy reflect the joint efforts of the

European Union and Ukraine to modernize Ukraine's energy infrastructure and approxi-

mate its energy legislation consistent with European Union standards. Conditionality and

externalization best describe the Europeanization of Ukraine's energy sector which

follows a "logic of consequences" model.

Ukraine is a key transit country for energy resources from Russia to the European

Union, particularly for gas where approximately 20 percent of the gas consumed in the

European Union is transited. Among the main objectives of European Union-Ukraine

energy cooperation since 2001 has been the need to guarantee the overall performance,

safety and security of the Ukrainian natural gas transit network.[174] On December, 1, 2005

the European Commission and Ukraine signed a Memorandum of Understanding on Co-

operation in the Field of Energy between the European Union and Ukraine.[175] The

Memorandum cites the "gradual convergence" of Ukraine's energy sector with the

European Union's internal energy market, "aiming ultimately at its integration," as a

---

[174]See, European Commission, Energy, External Dimension, Bilateral Co-operation, http://ec.europa.eu/energy/international/bilateral_cooperation/ukraine_en. htm (accessed March 20, 2012).

[175]See, *Memorandum of Understanding on Co-operation in the Field of Energy between the European Union and Ukraine*, December 1, 2005, http://ec.europa.eu/dgs/energy_transport/international/bilateral/ukraine/doc/mou_en_final_en.pdf (accessed March 20, 2012).

"shared priority" of the European Union and Ukraine.[176] The European Union and

Ukraine recognized that they share common energy policy challenges and that "enhanced

energy cooperation" would contribute to needed energy market reforms in Ukraine,

leading to an improved investment climate in Ukraine's energy sector.[177] The

Memorandum defined four roadmaps for bilateral cooperation: (1) nuclear safety, (2)

integration of electricity and gas markets, (3) security of energy supplies and transit of

hydrocarbons, and (4) safety and environmental standards in the coal sector.[178] A fifth

area concerning energy efficiency and renewable energies was added later.[179]

Annual progress reports assess the extent to which the parties to the Memorandum

succeeded in their joint energy strategy of bringing the energy markets of the European

Union and Ukraine closer together. The first progress report of October 18, 2006

addressed the establishment of working groups for each of the five areas of bilateral

cooperation and the European Union's provision of technical assistance and financial

support for oil and gas infrastructure projects. Significantly, the 2006 Progress Report

noted that "Ukraine is politically committed to meeting the requirements of European

Union Directives on minimum levels of oil stocks."[180] In addition, the working group on

---

[176]Ibid., 2.

[177]Ibid., 3.

[178]Ibid., 4.

[179]European Commission, *Joint EU-Ukraine Report, Implementation of the EU-Ukraine Memorandum of Understanding on Energy Cooperation during 2006*, October 18, 2006, 1, http://ec.europa.eu/energy/international/bilateral_cooperation/doc/ukraine/2006_10_progress_report.pdf (accessed March 20, 2012).

[180]Ibid., 2.

the integration of electricity and gas markets adopted a program that included

"verification of the Ukraine legislation and its implementation in order to determine

whether the existing and foreseen laws and regulations comply with the provisions of the

European Union's Electricity and Gas Directives."[181] The European Union, for its part,

pledged to "pave the way for Ukraine to participate as a full member of the Energy

Community Treaty" contingent on the satisfactory assessment of the level of nuclear

safety in all nuclear power plants operating in Ukraine.[182] The Energy Community deals

with electricity, natural gas, and petroleum products, and extends the European Union

internal energy market to South East Europe and beyond on the ground of a legally

binding framework.[183] It provides a stable investment environment based on the rule of

law, and ties the Contracting Parties together with the European Union. Through its

actions, the Energy Community contributes to security of supply in a wider Europe.[184]

---

[181]Ibid., 4.

[182]Ibid., 3. The *Treaty Establishing the Energy Community*, signed on October 25, 2005 by the European Community and then nine Contracting Parties from South East Europe, entered into force on July 1, 2006. The principles of the Treaty coincide with that of the European Steel and Coal Community, the genesis of the European Union. It strives to balance the commercial, political and social interests of all Parties by guaranteeing stable and continuous energy supply, and encouraging enhanced economic development and social stability. See, Energy Community, http://www.energy-community.org/portal/page/portal/ENC_HOME (accessed March 20, 2012).

[183]The Energy Community, *Legal Framework*, 2d ed., November 1, 2010, http://www.energy-community.org/pls/portal/ docs/808177.PDF (accessed March 20, 2012).

[184]Energy Community, http://www.energy-community.org/portal/page/portal/ENC_HOME/ENERGY_COMMUNITY/Facts_and_Figures (accessed March 20, 2012). The Parties to the Treaty are the European Union, on the one hand, and the Contracting Parties: Albania, Bosnia and Herzegovina, Croatia, former Yugoslav Republic of Macedonia, Moldova, Montenegro, Serbia and the United Nations Interim Administration Mission in Kosovo. Armenia, Georgia, Norway and Turkey take part as Observers.

The Second Joint European Union-Ukraine Report of September 14, 2007 noted progress on the "legal approximation in electricity and gas sectors" and that a draft Ukrainian law reinforcing the independence of Ukraine's National Energy Regulatory Committee[185] and opening up its gas and electricity markets was under examination by Ukraine's Parliament. The European Commission believed that once reviewed and adopted, the law would conform to the relevant European Union *acquis*.[186] A Third Report dated August 29, 2008, cited a three-stage Action Plan adopted by the Cabinet of Ministers of Ukraine in November 2007. Spanning the years 2008-2014, the Action Plan aims at moving Ukraine "away from the current wholesale electricity market model to a balancing market model." In addition, the Ministry of Fuel and Energy of Ukraine began modifying a draft law "On the Principles of the Natural Gas Market Functioning," for conformity with the European Union *acquis*.[187]

The years 2008 and 2009 marked a significant milestone in Ukraine's efforts to further integrate its energy policies with the European Union. The European Council adopted on July 15, 2008, a mandate for the European Commission to undertake

---

[185]See, National Electricity Regulatory Commission of Ukraine, http://www.nerc. gov.ua/ (accessed March 20, 2012).

[186]European Commission, *Second Joint EU-Ukraine Report, Implementation of the EU-Ukraine Memorandum of Understanding on Energy Cooperation during 2007*, September 14, 2007, 2, http://ec.europa.eu/energy/international/bilateral_cooperation/ doc/ukraine/2007_09_14_progress_report.pdf (accessed March 20, 2012).

[187]European Commission, *Third Joint EU-Ukraine Report, Implementation of the EU-Ukraine Memorandum of Understanding on Energy Cooperation during 2008*, August 29, 2008, 2, 3, http://ec.europa.eu/energy/international/bilateral_cooperation/doc/ ukraine/2008_08_29_progress_report.pdf (accessed March 20, 2012). Ukraine's National Energy Regulatory Committee began preparing the implementation of the first stage of the Action Plan the following year, 2009.

negotiations with Ukraine on its accession to the Energy Community which included

commitments for the gradual convergence with European Union internal energy market

rules. Negotiations began in November 2008, and included discussions on a time

schedule for Ukraine's implementation of the relevant European Union legislative acts.[188]

The European Commission assisted Ukraine in drafting a Law on Gas Market Operation

which was finalized in conformity with the European Union Gas Directive (2003/55/EC)

in September 2009 and adopted by the *Verkhovna Rada*. The gas law allowed for the

conclusion of negotiations concerning Ukraine's accession to the Energy Community on

October 7, 2009.[189] The Ministerial Council of the Energy Community approved the

accession of Ukraine as a Contracting Party to the Energy Community on December 18,

2009.[190] A subsequent Protocol signed September 24, 2010, provided a timetable for

Ukraine to implement various energy-related legislation of the *acquis communautaire*.[191]

Ukraine's Parliament adopted the Law on Ratification of the Protocol on Ukraine's

accession to the Treaty establishing the Energy Community on December 15, 2010 and

formally acceded to the Energy Community on February 1, 2011. Ukraine's joining

---

[188]European Commission, *Fourth Joint EU-Ukraine Report, Implementation of the EU-Ukraine Memorandum of Understanding on Energy Cooperation during 2009*, December 4, 2009, 2, http://ec.europa.eu/energy/international/bilateral_cooperation/doc/ukraine/2009_12_04_report.pdf (accessed March 20, 2012).

[189]Ibid., 3.

[190]Decision of the Ministerial Council of the Energy Community of 18 December 2009 approving the accession of Ukraine to the Energy Community Treaty (Decision 2009/04/MC-EnC), http://www.energy-community.org/pls/portal/docs/728177.PDF (accessed March 20, 2012).

[191]Protocol Concerning the Accession of Ukraine to the Treaty Establishing the Energy Community, September 24, 2010, http://www.energy-community.org/pls/portal/docs/728177.PDF (accessed March 20, 2012).

doubled the size and tripled the population of the Energy Community. More importantly, it marked a decisive step in further integrating Ukraine's energy sector into that of the European Union.

At a Joint European Union-Ukraine International Investment Conference on the Modernisation of Ukraine's Gas Transit System held in Brussels on March 23, 2009, Ukraine confirmed its intention regarding gas market reforms. On that occasion, Ukraine signed a joint declaration with the European Commission, the European Investment Bank, the European Bank for Reconstruction and Development, and the World Bank in which Ukraine expressed its intention to gradually integrate into the single energy market of the European Union via its membership in the Energy Community.[192] In addition, Ukraine adopted its law, "On the Principles of Functioning of the Natural Gas Market," in July 2010. The European Commission assessed the law to be "a sound basis for starting to align the Ukrainian gas market to European standards"[193] and pledged technical assistance to the Ministry of Fuel and Energy of Ukraine to further the process of legislative approximation in line with the European Union's energy *acquis*.[194]

---

[192]Joint EU-Ukraine International Investment Conference on the Modernisation of Ukraine's Gas Transit System, Joint Declaration, http://eeas.europa.eu/energy/events/ eu_ukraine_2009/joint_declaration_en.pdf (accessed March 20, 2012). Prime Minister Yulia Tymoshenko signed for the Government of Ukraine.

[193]European Commission, *Fifth Joint EU-Ukraine Report, Implementation of the EU-Ukraine Memorandum of Understanding on Energy Cooperation during 2010 November 22, 2010*, 3, http://ec.europa.eu/energy/international/bilateral_cooperation/doc/ ukraine/2010_11_22_report.pdf (accessed March 20, 2012).

[194]Ibid. See, Ministry of Fuel and Energy of Ukraine, http://mpe.kmu.gov.ua/fuel/ control/uk/index (accessed March 20, 2012).

Ukraine and the European Commission signed the sixth and most recent progress report of the Memorandum on Energy Cooperation on March 22, 2012.[195] The report acknowledges Ukraine's efforts in approximating its energy policies and laws with that of the European Union and recognizes Ukraine's initiative in revising its Energy Strategy to 2030. The European Commission expressed its commitment to provide financial support and technical assistance to ensure that Ukraine's new Energy Strategy is both "comprehensive and sustainable," that it "reinforces Ukraine's energy security," and that it accounts for the "commitments Ukraine entered into when joining the Energy Community."[196] The commitments refer to the timetable contained in the September 2010 Protocol Concerning the Accession of Ukraine to the Treaty Establishing the Energy Community which outlined the various energy-related legislation of the *acquis* that Ukraine is obligated to implement within the coming years. The Sixth Progress Report is the first signed by Ukraine as a member of the Energy Community. Commenting on the present state of Ukraine-European Union energy cooperation, Yuriy Boyko, Minister of Energy and Coal Industry of Ukraine, stated that Ukraine is "generally satisfied with our cooperation and believe that it is developing positively."[197] Ulrich Benterbusch, Director of Global Energy Dialogue at the International Energy

---

[195]European Commission, *Sixth Joint EU-Ukraine Report, Implementation of the EU-Ukraine Memorandum of Understanding on Energy Cooperation during 2011* March 22, 2012, http://ec.europa.eu/energy/international/bilateral_cooperation/doc/ukraine/2012_03_22_mou_progress_report6.pdf (accessed March 25, 2012).

[196]Ibid., 1.

[197]See, Ministry of Fuel and Energy of Ukraine, http://mpe.kmu.gov.ua/fuel/control/uk/publish/article;jsessionid=14697DA436379F320870064D79F0AD54?art_id=219245&cat_id=35109 (accessed March 25, 2012).

Agency (IEA), and Graham White, Team Leader for a forthcoming IEA review of Ukraine's energy policies acknowledged "Ukraine's strong political commitment to develop conventional and unconventional gas resources" and "the need to co-operate with the private sector and external players, such as the European Union."[198] The IEA commended Ukraine which has "shown progress through new legislation on the energy sector and a commitment to implementing the European Union Energy Community Treaty."[199]

Brief mention must be made of the Agreement between the European Atomic Energy Community and the Cabinet of Ministers of Ukraine for Co-operation in the Peaceful Uses of Nuclear Energy signed in Kyiv on April 28, 2005, and which entered into force on September 1, 2006.[200] The Agreement provides a framework for co-operation between the European Union and Ukraine in the peaceful uses of nuclear energy with a view to strengthening the overall relationship between the two. Ukraine and the European Union have achieved satisfactory progress in nuclear cooperation as

---

[198]International Energy Agency, "Ukraine has great potential to increase its energy security, says IEA's Director of Global Energy Dialogue," March 2, 2012, http://www. iea.org/index_info.asp?id=2392 (accessed March 25, 2012). The IEA review of Ukraine's energy policies is due to be published toward the end of 2012.

[199]Ibid. Benterbusch added that "Ukraine has great potential to increase its energy security, create jobs, foster economic growth and modernise its energy infrastructure by focusing on five priority areas: developing a comprehensive energy strategy; improving energy efficiency and district heating; increasing production of oil and gas; re-structuring the energy sector and introducing fair, predictable and competitive legislation; and promoting more private and foreign investments into the energy sector."

[200]*Agreement between the European Atomic Energy Community and the Cabinet of Ministers of Ukraine for Co-operation in the Peaceful Uses of Nuclear Energy*, April 28, 2005, http://ec.europa.eu/world/agreements/downloadFile.do?fullText=yes&treaty Trans Id=10181 (accessed March 20, 2012).

evidenced by the European Union's support for Ukraine's accession to the Energy Community Treaty following Ukraine's attaining of an appropriate level of nuclear safety in all of its nuclear power plants. There are at present 15 working nuclear reactors in Ukraine, generating 47 percent of the country's electricity. Ukraine remains committed to nuclear power, and is building two more reactors and planning as many as 11 more by 2030, as it seeks to reduce its dependence on energy from Russia, particularly in light of the disputes over gas in 2006 and 2009.[201]

As the annual progress reports on the Memorandum of Understanding on Co-operation in the Field of Energy between the European Union and Ukraine indicate, Ukraine continues to adopt measures integrating its energy laws and policies with those of the European Union. In addition to the appeal of access to the internal market, the European Union, for its part, has been able to leverage technical assistance and financial support towards making Ukraine's energy sector, particularly its gas market, more efficient and transparent. With approximately 20 percent of the gas consumed in the European Union transiting through Ukraine, the European Union recognized the need to commit Ukraine to a meaningful dialogue of energy cooperation beginning with the Memorandum of Understanding on Co-operation in the Field of Energy between the European Union and Ukraine of 2005. Arguably, the European Union initiated the process of Europeanizing Ukraine's energy sector, particularly its electricity and gas markets, but Ukraine has been quick to embrace the process. Evidence supporting the

---

[201]BBC News, *Nuclear Europe: Country Guide*, April 15, 2009, http://news. bbc.co.uk/2/hi/europe/4713398.stm (accessed March 20, 2012). See also, Ministry of Fuel and Energy of Ukraine, http://mpe.kmu.gov.ua/fuel/ control/uk/index (accessed March 20, 2012).

Europeanization of Ukraine's energy sector is the signing of the Protocol of September 2010 committing Ukraine to implement various energy-related legislation of the *acquis communautaire*, the legislation adopted in support of its successful accession to the Energy Community in 2011, and most recently, Ukraine's initiative in revising its Energy Strategy to 2030 to reflect approximation with the European Union energy *acquis*.

The direct method of conditionality, in the form of the technical and financial support provided by the European Union, and the indirect method of externalization, in the form of Ukraine looking to the European Union for comprehensive expertise in modernizing and improving its energy sector, are the two mechanisms that best describe the process of Europeanization underway within Ukraine in this area. Similar to Ukraine's economic integration, energy cooperation between the European Union and Ukraine follows Schimmelfennig's "logic of consequences" model. Ukraine's increased cooperation with the European Union in the area of energy not only approximates its domestic legislation to that of the energy *acquis*, it enables Ukraine to reduce its dependence on energy from Russia. This is no inconsiderable consequence, particularly in light of their disputes over gas in 2006 and 2009. Should Ukraine's efforts at legislative reform and increased energy cooperation with the European Union falter, Ukraine may face even greater financial dependency on its Slavic big brother.[202]

---

[202]See, Ildar Gazizullin and Larion Lozovyy, *Ukraine's Gas Market: Europeanization and the Russian Factor,* International Centre for Policy Studies (Kyiv: United States Agency for International Development, 2011), 5, http://www.icps.com.ua/files/articles/66/65/Gas%20Options_en_14_10.pdf (accessed March 20, 2012): "Ukraine's position in gas negotiations with Russia is weak. Its highly inefficient economy, a soviet-era policy of subsidizing residential utilities and the general lack of transparency in its gas sector are the leading factors underlying this weakness . . . The weak financial state of Ukraine's energy sector is forcing the country to continue to yield to Russian interests

Judicial Reform: Ukraine's Legislative Initiatives and the Council of Europe's Venice Commission

Among the main challenges of post-communist Ukraine has been building an independent judiciary within a democratic political system consistent with the doctrine of separation of powers. Indeed, the reform of the judiciary has been one of the major commitments undertaken by Ukraine since it joined the Council of Europe on November 9, 1995. Arguably Ukraine is undergoing the process of Europeanization in the area of judicial reform with the Council of Europe providing much needed support. Ukraine has long recognized the need to reform its judiciary, as well as modernize its criminal law and procedure, in an effort to achieve European standards. Ukraine's record of success in Europeanizing its judiciary and achieving reform has been somewhat spotty, however.

The mechanism of externalization may describe Ukraine's recent efforts at judicial reform. Ukraine has assumed the initiative over the course of several years by submitting various draft legislation to the European Commission for Democracy through Law (Venice Commission), an advisory body of the Council of Europe, for review and comment in an effort to ensure that the laws adopted by the *Verkhovna Rada* are consistent with European standards. The mechanism of conditionality is also at play. Incentives of increased political and economic integration promised by the Association Agreement and DCFTA are linked to Ukraine's progress in achieving judicial reform and embracing more fully the European core value of democracy under the rule of law. Ukraine's efforts follow a "logic of consequences" model since further progress

---

in order to receive concessions on the price of imported natural gas . . . The best option for Kyiv could be to institute European-style regulation on its gas market, which would reduce the risks attached to any increase in stakes in the market by Russian or other gas companies because they will be forced to compete with each other."

involving the Association Agreement is dependent on Ukraine ensuring an independent

judiciary which can only be achieved by reforming Ukrainian legislation. The "logic of

appropriateness" mechanisms of socialization and imitation are less at work in Ukraine.

These models emphasize Ukraine's identification with the European Union, but interpret

Ukraine's efforts at judicial reform as occurring independent of any material incentive or

reward. The Joint European Union-Ukraine Action Plan and the recently drafted

Association Agreement and DCFTA provide Ukraine with sufficient material incentives

such as increased access to the single market and removal of trade barriers. Such

incentives reflect the "logic of consequences" model identifying Ukraine's efforts at

Europeanizing its judiciary. It is evident, however, that Ukraine needs to take greater

steps at achieving judicial reform if it is to advance along the path of Europeanization.

Ukraine submitted draft laws on the Status of Judges and the Law on the Judiciary

to the Venice Commission for review and comment in October 2006.[203] The laws were

prepared with the general aim of fulfilling European standards on the judiciary, in line

with the Council of Europe's Recommendation of the Committee of Ministers to Member

States on the Independence, Efficiency and Role of Judges,[204] and the European Charter

---

[203] See, Council of Europe, European Commission for Democracy through Law
(Venice Commission), *Draft Law on the Judiciary of Ukraine* CDL(2006)096, Opinion
no. 401/2006, December 4, 2006, and *Draft Law on the Status of Judges of Ukraine*
CDL(2006)097, Opinion no. 402/2006, December 4, 2006. See the revised versions with
comparative tables showing amendments to the drafts: CDL(2007)040, Opinion no.
401/2006, March 6, 2007 and CDL(2007)039, Opinion no. 401/2006, March 6, 2007,
http://www.venice.coe.int/docs/2006/CDL(2006)096-e.asp (accessed March 20, 2012).

[204] See, Council of Europe, *Recommendation No. R (94)12 of the Committee of
Ministers to Member States on the Independence, Efficiency and Role of Judges,*
Strasbourg, October 13, 1994, https://wcd.coe.int/com.instranet.InstraServlet?command=
com.instranet.CmdBlobGet&InstranetImage=534553&SecMode=1&DocId=514386&Us
age=2 (accessed March 20, 2012).

on the Statute for Judges.[205] In March 2007, the Venice Commission issued its *Opinion on the Draft Law on the Judiciary and the Draft Law on the Status of Judges of Ukraine.*[206] The *Opinion* addresses a number of areas, including judicial immunity from external pressure or influence, Ukraine's court system, the appointment of judges, judicial promotions, disciplinary liability and dismissal of judges. Although the Venice Commission found that the "general rules are in line with European standards,"[207] they nonetheless provided a great deal of critical comment and a comprehensive list of recommendations for improving the draft laws. By way of example, the *Opinion* cites the need to curb the discretionary powers of the President of Ukraine by limiting him to the verification of whether the necessary procedure had been followed. In addition, the Venice Commission urged the need for "clear and stringent criminal sanctions . . . to protect judges against external pressure."[208]

---

[205]Council of Europe, European Commission for Democracy through Law (Venice Commission), *Comments on the Draft Law on the Judiciary and the Draft Law on the Status of Judges of Ukraine*, by Ms. Hanna Suchochka, March 6, 2007, CDL (2007) 035, Opinion no. 401.2006, http://www.venice.coe.int/docs/2007/CDL(2007)035-e.pdf (accessed March 20, 2012). See also, Council of Europe, *European Charter on the Statute for Judges and Explanatory Memorandum*, Strasbourg, July 8-10, 1998, http://www.coe.int/t/dghl/monitoring/greco/evaluations/round4/European-Charter-on-Statute-of-Judges_EN.pdf (accessed March 20, 2012).

[206]Council of Europe, European Commission for Democracy through Law (Venice Commission), *Opinion on the Draft Law on the Judiciary and the Draft Law on the Status of Judges of Ukraine*, adopted by the Venice Commission at its 70th Plenary Session, Venice (16-17 March 2007), CDL-AD(2007)003, Opinion no. 401/2006, March 20, 2007, http://www.venice.coe.int/docs/2007/CDL-AD(2007)003-e.pdf (accessed March 20, 2012).

[207]Ibid., 4.

[208]Ibid., 17-18.

In the months following the March 2007 *Opinion*, Ukrainian authorities amended

the draft laws, ultimately consolidating them into one comprehensive draft law: "On the

Judicial System and the Status of Judges." In July 2009, the Ukrainian Ministry of Justice

requested an opinion from the Venice Commission on the newly consolidated draft law

which had been prepared and approved by the *Verkhovna Rada's* Judiciary Committee in

June 2008.[209] Similar to the earlier March 2007 *Opinion*, a March 2010 *Joint Opinion*

adopted by the Venice Commission and the Directorate of Co-operation within the

Directorate General of Human Rights and Legal Affairs of the Council of Europe,

provided critical comments on a number of areas: the system of courts, appointment of

judges, disciplinary liability and dismissal, judicial self-government, and judicial

training.[210] The Venice Commission concluded its 27-page *Joint Opinion* by noting that

although the amended draft law followed some of its earlier recommendations and that

most of the changes made were "positive and should be regarded as improvements" the

---

[209]Council of Europe, European Commission for Democracy through Law
(Venice Commission), *Draft Law on the Judicial System and the Status of Judges of
Ukraine*, CDL-AD(2009)111, Opinion no. 550/2009, September 21, 2009, http://www.
venice.coe. int/docs/2009/CDL(2009)111-e.pdf (accessed March 20, 2012). Ukraine's
Ministry of Justice subsequently submitted a revised version of its *Draft Law of Ukraine
on the Judiciary and the Status of Judges* to the Venice Commission on June 15, 2010.
See, CDL-AD(2010)064, Opinion no. 588/2010, http://www.venice.coe.int/ docs/2010/
CDL(2010)064-e.pdf (accessed March 20, 2012).

[210]Council of Europe, European Commission for Democracy through Law
(Venice Commission), *Joint Opinion on the Draft Law on the Judicial System and the
Status of Judges of Ukraine*, adopted by the Venice Commission and the Directorate of
Co-operation within the Directorate General of Human Rights and Legal Affairs of the
Council of Europe at its 82nd Plenary Session, Venice (12-13 March 2010), Opinion no.
550/2009, http://www. venice.coe.int/docs/ 2010/CDL-AD(2010)003-e.asp (accessed
March 20, 2012).

draft law did not address the more "serious reservations."[211] Major problems cited in the

Joint Opinion include a system of appointment and removal of judges that "appears to

allow politicisation of the process in a way which is difficult to reconcile with the

requirement of separation of powers and the independence of the judiciary." The *Joint*

Opinion criticized the "complicated" system of judicial self-government for having too

many institutions that could become "an obstacle for building a real self-government and

the scope of 'judicial politics' seems enormous."[212] The Venice Commission was most

critical, however, of Ukraine's Constitution which contained provisions that were "an

obstacle for an independent Judiciary in line with European standards."[213] Ultimately the

Venice Commission and the Directorate General of Human Rights and Legal Affairs of

the Council of Europe recommended substantial changes to the draft law, some of which

required constitutional reform.

Despite the critical comments contained in the March 2010 *Joint Opinion*, the

Verkhovna Rada adopted the law on July 7, 2010 without implementing most of the

Council of Europe's recommendations; President Yanukovych signed the law on July

27.[214] The law includes a number of positive provisions that aid judicial independence,

---

[211]Ibid., 25.

[212]Ibid., 25-26. "The dispersal of powers through many bodies seems to lead to a potentially confusing situation where different bodies would exercise the same powers."

[213]Ibid., 25. "The Commission recommends to confine judicial reform not to the legislative level but to undertake a profound constitutional reform, aiming to lay down the solid foundation for a modern and efficient judiciary in full compliance with European standards."

[214]Council of Europe, European Commission for Democracy through Law (Venice Commission), Law of Ukraine No 2453-VI, On the Judiciary and the Status of Judges, adopted by the *Verkhovna Rada* on 7 July 2010, CDL(201)084, Opinion no.

including improvements to the selection process of judges, inclusion of the State

Judiciary Administration within the judiciary itself, improvements to court financing,

provisions for training judges, and a reduction of the number of justices of the Supreme

Court from 80 to 20.[215] On the other hand, some provisions conflict with the principle of

an independent judiciary. For example, under the new law the president of Ukraine can

create and abolish courts of general jurisdiction, based on the recommendation of the

justice minister following a proposal from the chief judge of the relevant high specialized

court. Ukraine's constitution, however, does not give such a power to the president.[216] In

addition, the law significantly reduces the authority of the Supreme Court and increases

the authority of the High Council of Justice, a body criticized for lacking

independence.[217] Ukraine's constitution recognizes the Supreme Court as the highest

judicial body within the courts of general jurisdiction. Pursuant to the new law, however,

the high specialized courts decide whether to submit a case for further review to the

---

588/2010, http://www.venice.coe.int/docs/2010/CDL(2010)084-e.pdf (accessed March 20, 2012).

[215]Bohdan A. Futey, "The Suppression of an Independent judiciary in Ukraine," Kyiv Post, December 27, 2011, http://www.kyivpost.com/news/opinion/op_ed/detail/ 119708/ (accessed March 20, 2012). See also, Peter Solomon, Jr., "Yanukovych's Judicial Reform: Power & Policy," *Ukraine Watch*, March 2, 2011, http://ukrainewatch. wordpress.com/2011/03/02/yanukovychs-judicial-reform-power-policy/ (accessed March 20, 2012).

[216]Ibid.

[217]See, Human Rights Watch, *World Report 2011: Ukraine*, Events of 2010, http://www.hrw.org/world-report-2011/ukraine (accessed March 20, 2012).

Supreme Court. Its power essentially vanishes under this new law; Ukraine's Supreme Court can no longer choose the cases it hears.[218]

Within weeks of his February 2010 election victory, President Yanukovych chaired a meeting of a working group on judicial reform in which he stated that "Ukraine has obligations concerning adapting Ukrainian legislation to European standards."[219] During an August 2010 swearing-in ceremony of newly appointed judges, Yanukovych declared that large-scale judicial reform in Ukraine would guarantee the fairness and independence of the courts.[220] Moreover, he acknowledged that one of the tasks of judicial reform is to bring Ukraine's judicial system in line with the standards and regulations of the Council of Europe.[221] Contrary to achieving his goal of attaining a judicial system in line with European standards, the law, On the Judiciary and the Status of Judges, adopted by the *Verkhovna Rada* in July 2010, appears to have raised concerns

---

[218]Futey, "The Suppression of an Independent judiciary in Ukraine." "When Ukraine's constitution was first adopted in 1996, many, including the Venice Commission, commended Ukraine for enacting a document that guaranteed human rights. Now, however, Ukraine finds itself in the unenviable position of having its actions questioned and condemned by those same observers."

[219]For-ua.com, "President Holding meeting of Working Group on Judicial Reform," March 25, 2010, http://en.for-ua.com/news/2010/03/25/181309.html (accessed March 20, 2012). See also, Sevrugin "Yanukovych calls for judicial reform: We cannot continue to disgrace the country," March 25, 2010, http://news.sevrugin.com/node/1190 (accessed March 20, 2012).

[220]Kyiv Post, "Yanukovych Outlines Goals for Judicial Reform in Ukraine," August 2010, http://www.kyivpost.com/news/politics/detail/78745/ (accessed March 20, 2012). "The courts are obliged to be honest, and have no right to support any [political] forces, apart from the law and the legitimate interests of our citizens."

[221]Ibid.

of the increasing politicization of Ukraine's judiciary and the increasing assumption of control over the courts by Ukraine's executive.

In recommending changes to the draft law, On the Judicial System and the Status of Judges of Ukraine, in its March 2010 *Joint Opinion,* the Venice Commission mentioned the need for constitutional reform. Several months later, it adopted its *Opinion on the Constitutional Situation in Ukraine* at its 85th Plenary Session, on December 17-18, 2010.[222] The report noted that Ukraine's Constitution, adopted on June 28, 1996, established a presidential-parliamentary type of government institutional regime; subsequent amendments in December 2004 increased the parliamentary features of Ukraine's political system.[223] On October 1, 2010, however, the Constitutional Court of

---

[222]Council of Europe, European Commission for Democracy through Law (Venice Commission), *Opinion on the Constitutional Situation in Ukraine*, adopted by the Venice Commission at its 85th Plenary Session, Venice (17-18 December 2012), Opinion no. 599/2010, http://www.venice.coe.int/docs/2010/CDL-AD(2010)044-e.pdf (accessed March 20, 2012).

[223]For example, the 2004 amendments expanded the powers of the *Verkhovna Rada,* which gained the right to appoint the prime minister, the defense and foreign ministers under a motion from the president, as well as other government members under a motion from the prime minister. The 1996 Constitution, by contrast, allowed the president to pick the prime minister and cabinet ministers, and had shorter parliamentary terms of only four years, compared to five years under the amendments introduced in 2004, and now repealed. In addition, under the 1996 Constitution, the president is elected for five years, nominates candidates for prime minister (for parliamentary ratification) and appoints cabinet ministers, has the right to dismiss government without parliamentary approval and can cancel any government resolution. See, Kyiv Post, "Update: Return to 1996 Constitution Strengthens President, Raises Legal Questions," October 1, 2010, http://www.kyivpost.com/news/politics/detail/84619/ (accessed March 20, 2012); Kyiv Post, "Political Analysts: Cancelation of 2004 Political Reform May Deepen Split in Ukraine," August 25, 2010, http://www.kyivpost.com/news/politics/detail/79746/ (accessed March 20, 2012).

Ukraine overturned the 2004 amendments, considering them unconstitutional.[224] In reviewing the judgment of the Constitutional Court, the members of the Venice Commission considered it "highly unusual that far-reaching constitutional amendments, including the change of the political system of the country--from a parliamentary system to a parliamentary-presidential one--are declared unconstitutional by a decision of the Constitutional Court after a period of 6 years."[225] Acknowledging "that neither the Constitution of Ukraine nor the Law on the Constitutional Court provide for a time-limit for contesting the constitutionality of a law before the Constitutional Court of Ukraine," the Commission, nonetheless pointed out that "Constitutional Courts are bound by the Constitution and do not stand above it, *such decisions raise important questions of democratic legitimacy and the rule of law.*"[226] In addition, the Commission addressed the need for Ukraine to take further steps in order to bring the new constitutional framework in line with European standards and norms.

> The fundamental problem in Ukraine for more than a decade has been dysfunctional institutions, a lack of checks and balances especially with respect to the powers of the President, constant clashes between the State organs and intense disputes over the Constitution. Considering current political realities, the strengthening of the powers of the President can become an obstacle for building genuine democratic structures and may eventually lead to an excessively authoritarian system . . . Therefore, the present constitutional situation and the 30 September Judgment should not be used as a reason to avoid a comprehensive constitutional reform called for by, *inter alia*, the Parliamentary Assembly of the

---

[224]See, Kyiv Post, "Constitutional Court to Issue Ruling on 2004 Political Reform on Friday," September 30, 2010, http://www.kyivpost.com/news/politics/detail/84452/ (accessed March 20, 2012).

[225]Ibid., 6. For an English translation of Ukraine's Constitution see, Viktor Yanukovych, President of Ukraine, http://www.president.gov.ua/en/content/constitution. html (accessed March 20, 2012).

[226]Ibid., emphasis added.

Council of Europe[227] and the European Union.[228] It is clear that the current constitutional framework based on a ruling of the Constitutional Court does notenjoy sufficient legitimacy, which only the regular constitutional procedure for constitutional amendments in the *Verkhovna Rada* can ensure.[229]

The reinstatement of the 1996 version of the Constitution by the 2010 judgment of the Constitutional Court of Ukraine raised questions of the legitimacy of past actions, since the institutions of Ukraine worked for several years on the basis of constitutional rules later declared unconstitutional. In addition, overturning the 2004 amendments raised questions of legitimacy with respect to President Yanukovych and members of the *Verkhovna Rada* elected under constitutional rules that are no longer recognized as valid. This is significant, for as the members of the Venice Commission point out, "[t]he President of Ukraine, as from this judgment, enjoys far more powers than could be foreseen by the voters when he was elected. The working of the main state organs is now based on rules changed by a court and not on rules changed by the *Verkhovna Rada*, as a democratically legitimate body."[230] At the time of the overturning of the 2004 amendments, former prime minister and opposition leader, Yulia Tymoshenko, strongly criticized the move, calling it a "usurpation of state power" and said that "October 1 would go down in Ukrainian history as the day democracy was murdered and a

---

[227]See, European Parliament, Resolution of 25 November 2010 on Ukraine (Doc. P7_TA-PROV (2010)0444), http://www.europarl.europa.eu/document/activities/cont/ 201011/ 20101129ATT02496/20101129ATT02496EN.pdf (accessed March 20, 2012).

[228]See, Joint statement at the European Union-Ukraine summit, held in Brussels on 22 November 2010 (MEMO/10/600), http://europa.eu/rapid/pressReleasesAction.do? reference=MEMO/10/600 (accessed March 20, 2012).

[229]Venice Commission, *Opinion on the Constitutional Situation in Ukraine*, 10.

[230]Ibid., 11.

dictatorship installed."[231] The members of the Venice Commission concluded their report

by encouraging Ukrainian authorities "to introduce additional mechanisms and

procedures of parliamentary control over the actions and intentions of the executive," and

that "constitutional reform should also include changes in the provisions on the judiciary

aiming at 'laying down a solid foundation for a modern and efficient judiciary in full

compliance with European standards.'"[232] A few months after the Venice Commission

issued its *Opinion on the Constitutional Situation in Ukraine*, the European Commission

issued its *Joint Staff Working Paper on the Implementation of the European Neighbour-

hood Policy in 2010*.[233] The European Commission cited the work of the Venice

Commission noting their recommendation that Ukrainian authorities should "engage in a

comprehensive process of constitutional reform based on established procedures and

involving all the relevant players."[234]

Responding in part to the shared criticisms, President Yanukovych signed a

decree creating a Commission on Strengthening Democracy and the Rule of Law in

---

[231]See, Kyiv Post, "Update: Return to 1996 Constitution Strengthens President, Raises Legal Questions," October 1, 2010, http://www.kyivpost.com/news/politics/detail/84619/ (accessed March 20, 2012).

[232]Ibid., 12, citing Council of Europe, European Commission for Democracy through Law (Venice Commission), *Joint Opinion on the Draft Law on the Judicial System and the Status of Judges of Ukraine*, adopted by the Venice Commission at its 82nd Plenary Session, Venice (12-13 March 2010), Opinion no. 550/2009, http://www.venice.coe.int/docs/2010/CDL-AD(2010)003-e.asp (accessed March 20, 2012).

[233]European Commission, Joint Staff Working Paper, Implementation of the European Neighbourhood Policy in 2010, Country Report on: Ukraine, May 25, 2011, COM(2011) 303, SEC(2011) 646, http://ec.europa.eu/world/enp/pdf/progress2011/sec_11_646_en.pdf (accessed March 20, 2012).

[234]Ibid., 4.

Ukraine on November 5, 2010.[235] The Commission is charged with the "preparation of

proposals regarding attaining compliance of the Constitution of Ukraine with European

standards and values" based on the recommendations of the Venice Commission.[236]

Critics of Yanukovych may dismiss this Commission as amounting to little more than a

publicity campaign aimed at fending off increased attacks against Ukraine's political

leadership which many accuse of manipulating laws to strengthen the presidential power

base. Whether this Commission will have any significant impact on judicial reform

remains to be seen. At the very least, it is an acknowledgment by Ukraine that reform is

necessary within its judicial and legislative arenas. The effort may be seen as a welcome

attempt signaling an awareness of the significance of democracy under the rule of law.

The following year, Thomas Hammarberg, Commissioner for Human Rights for

the Council of Europe visited Ukraine in November 2011, and found that "systemic

deficiencies in the functioning of the Ukrainian judicial system seriously threaten human

rights."[237] He stated that Ukraine's judicial system "is still vulnerable to external

---

[235]KyivPost, "Yanukovych sets up commission to strengthen democracy, rule of law," November 5, 2010, http://www.kyivpost.com/news/politics/detail/88936/#ixzz1u6GAf0Ce (accessed March 20, 2012). Presidential Decree No. 1015/2010 reads: "In order to unite the efforts of government agencies, political parties, NGOs, and other civil society institutions in strengthening democracy and the rule of law, and in line with clause 28, part 1, of Article 106 of the Constitution of Ukraine, I order the formation of a commission on strengthening democracy and the rule of law as an advisory body."

[236]Cited in Opinion On the Concept Paper on the Establishment and Functioning of a Constitutional Assembly of Ukraine, adopted by the Venice Commission at its 86th Plenary Session, Venice, March 25-26, 2011, Opinion no. 618/2011, http://www.venice.coe.int/docs/2011/CDL-AD(2011)002-e.pdf (accessed March 20, 2012).

[237]Interfax-Ukraine, "Council of Europe human rights commissioner: Ukraine's judicial system needs independence," Kyiv Post, February 23, 2012, http://www.kyivpost.com/ news/nation/detail/123012/ (accessed March 20, 2012). Hammerberg visited Ukraine 19-26 November 2011.

interference, including of a political nature" and that significant measures are needed "to increase the transparency of the judicial system and make it more open to public scrutiny."[238] He stressed the need for urgent reform of Ukraine's judicial system calling on Ukrainian authorities to establish fair procedures and criteria related to the appointment and dismissal of judges, including the application of disciplinary measures. Moreover, he expressed concern about the "imbalance between the defense and the prosecution" and that there was evidence of "abusive prosecutions, harassment, and other forms of pressure on lawyers."[239]

Approximately six months before Hammarberg's visit to Ukraine, senior officials participating in a joint committee of the European Union-Ukraine Association Agenda on May 20, 2011, agreed upon a list of priorities including those in the areas of democracy, rule of law, human rights and fundamental freedoms. Among these priorities is the requirement that Ukraine "ensure the independence of the judiciary and the effectiveness of the courts and of the prosecution as well as of law enforcement agencies." The list of priorities calls for Ukraine to reform its judiciary and court system "so as to further strengthen the independence, impartiality, and professionalism of the judiciary and courts."[240] Commenting on the trial and conviction of former Prime Minister Yulia

---

[238]Ibid. "Decisive action is needed on several fronts to remove the factors which render judges vulnerable and weaken their independence. The authorities should carefully look into any allegations of improper political or other influence or interference in the work of judicial institutions and ensure effective remedies."

[239]Ibid.

[240]European Union External Action Service, Ukraine, "List of the EU-Ukraine Association Agenda priorities for 2011-2012," Agreed by the Joint Committee at Senior Official's Level of EU-Ukraine Association Agenda on 20 May 2011. See, http://www.

Tymoshenko at a Ukraine-European Union summit in Kyiv in December 2011, European Council President Herman Van Rompuy expressed his concern "connected with a certain politicization of the judicial system in Ukraine. The Tymoshenko case proves this."[241]

Ukraine inherited a judicial system from that of the Soviet Union and the former Ukrainian Soviet Socialist Republic that was marred by many problems including a corrupt and politicized judiciary. Criminal proceedings, investigations, and court examination in criminal trials are regulated by *The Criminal Procedural Code of Ukraine*, which has not changed since 1962. In September 2011, one month before the criminal trial of his former political opponent, President Yanukovych commented that Ukraine's criminal procedure code was under revision for the first time since 1962, and acknowledged that many things now considered to be criminal acts should not be when the laws are rewritten. Yanukovych, however, did not speculate at that time on when the new laws might become effective.[242] Since his comments, a law decriminalizing a number of articles of the Ukrainian Criminal Code has come into force on January 17, 2012. Ukraine's *Verkhovna Rada*, however, voted down a bill decriminalizing Article

---

eeas.europa.eu/ukraine/docs/2011_12_eu_ukraine_priorities_en.pdf (accessed March 15, 2012).

[241]Kyiv Post, "Tymoshenko Case Shows Politicization of Ukraine's Judicial System," December 19, 2012, http://www.kyivpost.com/news/politics/detail/119234/ (accessed March 20, 2012).

[242]Kyiv Post, "Yanukovych Mum about Tymoshenko," September 20, 2011, http://www.kyivpost.com/news/politics/detail/113202/ (accessed March 20, 2012).

365 of the Criminal Code under which former Prime Minister Tymoshenko had been sentenced to imprisonment in October 2011.[243]

More recently, a draft Criminal Procedure Code proposed by Yanukovych is currently before the *Verkhovna Rada* and the current parliamentary majority anticipates that it may be adopted in 2012. If adopted, the new Criminal Procedure Code could support the revision of criminal cases including that of former Prime Minister Tymoshenko. In an interview in late February, Yanukovych commented that the criminal cases should be considered again "from the point of view of the new Criminal Procedure Code," and stated further that the Code "will comply with European standards."[244] Concerning the case of his political rival, Yanukovych stated that he is interested in finding the "right solution" and reviewing Tymoshenko's case according to "European standards."[245] With remarkable candor, Yanukovych admitted that the trial of Yulia Tymoshenko fell short of European standards. "From what Europeans say, I agree with the fact that Ukraine's legislation is imperfect and that the trial of Tymoshenko and others

---

[243]Kyiv Post, "Parliament Again Votes Down Proposal to Decriminalize 'Tymoshenko Article'," February 8, 2012, http://www.kyivpost.com/news/politics/detail/122050/ (accessed March 20, 2012).

[244]Kyiv Post, "Yanukovych Supports Revision of Tymoshenko's Criminal Case," February 25, 2012, http://www.kyivpost.com/news/politics/detail/123149/ (accessed March 20, 2012).

[245]Kyiv Post, "Ukraine's President Hints at Tymoshenko Reprieve," February 25, 2012, http://www.kyivpost.com/news/nation/detail/123156/ (accessed March 20, 2012). Yanukovych did not indicate exactly how changing the country's criminal code may affect Tymoshenko's case.

didn't meet European standards and principles. I absolutely agree with this."[246] It remains

to be seen whether Yanukovych is sincere in his comments concerning the compliance of

Ukrainian criminal procedure with European standards, and what actions he may take

regarding the fate of Yulia Tymoshenko. It may be that he is simply bluffing in an effort

to earn concessions from the European Union and appease the Ukrainian people in order

to strengthen his own authority as president of Ukraine. Notwithstanding Yanukovych's

pledge that Ukraine's laws and judicial system will be reformed to comply with European

standards, disapproval of the politicization of Ukraine's judiciary continues, as evidenced

by the criticism issued by the Council of Europe's Venice Commission and the European

Union's express concerns over the controversial Tymoshenko prosecution.

Whereas the European Union assumed a much more assertive role in assisting

Ukraine Europeanize in the areas of economic integration and energy cooperation, it has

been the Council of Europe, particularly the Venice Commission, which has worked most

closely with Ukraine's Ministry of Justice to reform Ukraine's judiciary.[247] Indeed the

Venice Commission has assisted Ukraine by issuing dozens of opinions and advisory

papers on draft legislation submitted by Ukrainian authorities since Ukraine became a

member of the Council of Europe in 1995. This is not to say, however, that the European

Union has not provided assistance to Ukraine in the field of judicial reform. In June 2008,

---

[246]Kyiv Post, "Trials of Tymoshenko, Other Officials Fall short of European Standards, Yanukovych Admits," February 25, 2012, http://www.kyivpost.com/news/ politics/detail/123159/ (accessed March 20, 2012).

[247]Most recently, the Venice Commission and Ukraine's *Verkhovna Rada* organized a roundtable on the implementation of a new law on parliamentary elections in Ukraine scheduled to be held later this year. See, Council of Europe, Venice Commission, Calendar of Events, http://www.venice.coe.int/ (accessed March 20, 2012).

the European Union and the Council of Europe initiated a three-year joint program

entitled: "Transparency and Efficiency of the Judicial System of Ukraine."[248] The stated

objective of the program was "[t]o assist with the establishment of an independent,

impartial, efficient and professional judiciary in Ukraine, and to ensure that the Ukrainian

judiciary is transformed into a transparent and fair judicial system that is accessible to all

citizens, working effectively and transparently vis-à-vis citizens and civil society."[249] The

program was instrumental in organizing roundtable discussions concerning draft

legislation intended to conform more closely to European standards and in assisting in the

training of judges and prosecutors.[250]

The findings and analysis based on the formal Comments and Opinions issued by

Venice Commission suggest a lack of consistency in Ukraine's effort at reforming its

judiciary to attain European standards. In the few areas that Ukraine has succeeded in

Europeanizing its judiciary, for example the selection and training of judges and

prosecutors, the mechanism of conditionality may best characterize Ukraine's approach

to Europeanization. The eventual signing of the Association Agreement and

implementation of the Deep and Comprehensive Free Trade Area are conditioned on

Ukraine's adopting necessary reforms aimed at ensuring the transparency of its judicial

---

[248] See, Council of Europe, Legal and Human Rights Capacity Building, http://www.coe.int/t/dghl/cooperation/capacitybuilding/projects/tejsu_en.asp (accessed March 20, 2012). The European Union funded 90 percent of the program.

[249] Ibid.

[250] Ibid. A major result achieved by the project is related to the drafting of the legislation on automatic case-management system in Ukrainian courts. See also, Norris Stussy, *Strenthening* (sic) *the Strategy for a National Court Case Management System,* USAID, Ukraine Rule of Law Project, June 25, 2008, http://pdf.usaid.gov/pdf_docs/PNADP158.pdf (accessed March 20, 2012).

system. By withholding its signature to the Association Agreement, however, the European Union is signaling to Ukraine that it needs to take stronger measures to reform its judiciary.

Similarly, the mechanism of externalization applies to Ukraine's efforts, albeit to a lesser extent. Attracted to the economic incentives offered by the Association Agreement and Free Trade Area, Ukraine acknowledges the need to reform its judiciary--as well as its criminal laws and procedures--and continues to engage the Council of Europe and the European Commission. Despite some improvements, Ukraine has been considerably less successful in Europeanizing its judiciary compared to its achievements in economic integration and energy cooperation. Ukraine may need to address more critically the costs of further Europeanization efforts within its judiciary and the benefits of closer political and economic association with the European Union. In this regard, Schimmelfennig's and Sedelmeier's "logic of consequences" model is most appropriate to describe Ukraine's limited efforts at Europeanizing its judiciary. The European Union may sign the Association Agreement, but only if Ukraine demonstrates its commitment to European values of a transparent judicial system and a democratic government under the rule of law.

CHAPTER 5

CONCLUSION

The results of this research suggest that Ukraine is undertaking the process of Europeanization in its economic and energy sectors, but to a lesser degree within its judiciary. Since the Orange Revolution, Ukraine has adopted substantial measures aimed at undertaking the process of Europeanization in the area of economic integration. The European Union initiated and encouraged Ukraine's efforts to Europeanize by entering into structured agreements, such as the 2005 Joint European Union-Ukraine Action Plan, and the 2009 Association Agenda, both of which offered Ukraine significant incentives to Europeanize by means of financial support and technical assistance. The success of Ukraine's efforts at undertaking the process of Europeanization is evident from the annual progress reports citing Ukraine's progress in reforming its domestic economic structures and approximating its economic legislation to that of the European Union's *acquis communautaire*. Conditionality and externalization best characterize Ukraine's efforts at Europeanizing it economic structures. The European Union established the conditions that Ukraine had to fulfill in order to receive the rewards of technical assistance, financial support and increasing institutional ties with the European Union. Ukraine reciprocated by adopting the necessary reforms in compliance with the provisions of the bilateral agreements, thus following a "logic of consequences" model.

The results further suggest that Ukraine has achieved similar success at Europeanizing its energy sector, cooperating with the European Union through such instruments as the 2005 Memorandum of Understanding on Co-operation in the Field of Energy. In recent years, Ukraine succeeded in adopting legislation consistent with the energy *acquis* of the European Union. This has allowed Ukraine to accede to the European Energy Community and sign a Protocol with the European Union committing Ukraine to implement various energy-related legislation of the *acquis communautaire*. In addition, Ukraine has taken the initiative to revise its Energy Strategy to 2030 to reflect approximation with European Union energy rules and policies. Conditionality and externalization characterize Ukraine's efforts at undertaking the process of Europeanization in its energy sector which follows a "logic of consequences" model.

Arguably Ukraine's motivation for undergoing Europeanization in the fields of economic integration and energy cooperation is twofold: removing trade barriers that will secure increased access to the 27-member state internal market and modernizing Ukraine's economic and energy infrastructures. In addition to being motivated by the promise of eventual membership in the European Union, Ukraine has been adopting domestic reforms and institutional changes because of the acknowledged appropriateness and legitimacy of the need for reform within Ukraine. Guided by the policies of the European Union's European Neighbourhood Policy and the Eastern Partnership project, Ukraine has undertaken the process of Europeanization in its economic and energy sectors.

On the other hand, Ukraine has not fully embraced the Europeanization of its judiciary. Despite qualified success in working with the Council of Europe's Venice Commission, Ukraine's commitment to an independent judiciary and the rule of law has been questioned by the Council of Europe and the European Union. This raises the issue of whether Ukraine is capable of meeting the basic criteria and conditions for seeking membership in the European Union. Ukraine and the European Union succeeded in negotiating an Association Agreement in late 2011, and this instrument promises to secure even closer political and economic ties between the two. Yet dissatisfaction caused by the absence of an independent judiciary and Ukraine's lack of commitment to the rule of law has since led the European Union to withhold signing the Association Agreement. This is characteristic of the mechanism of conditionality; the European Union holds the superior bargaining power and is able to withhold the rewards offered by the Association Agreement and Free Trade Area as a consequence of Ukraine's noncompliance in matters of judicial independence.

On March 29, 2012, Yulia Tymoshenko issued a statement from her prison cell at the Kachanivska penal colony in Kharkiv in which she asked the European Union to sign the Association Agreement with Ukraine. For Ukraine, signing the Association Agreement would be "a historical breakthrough towards the European dream" and give hope, freedom and dignified life to 47 million Ukrainians.[251] Declaring that "Yanukovych's government has nothing to do with Europe or democracy" she urged the European Union to initial the Agreement which will serve as "a serious and effective barrier" against Ukraine "sinking into the abyss of post-Soviet totalitarianism."[252] In addition to criticizing her political rival, Tymoshenko expressed her concern over the fate of Ukraine's European aspirations if the Association Agreement were not signed.

> A disrupted signing of the Agreement will mean a failure of Ukraine's European aspirations. It could become a tragedy that will overshadow Ukraine's future for many years to come. The Ukrainian authorities, disguised by European rhetoric,

---

[251]Kyiv Post, "Tymoshenko Asks EU to Sign Agreement to Save Ukraine From Totalitarianism," March 29, 2012, http://www.kyivpost.com/news/politics/detail/125147/ (accessed March 30, 2012).

[252]Ibid.

are hoping precisely that the Agreement will not be signed, so as to be able to say later: Europe does not want us, so we do not want it. But this is the position of the authorities; this is the position of a few people who temporarily represent our state internationally.[253]

The following day, March 30, the European Union granted Tymoshenko's request--at least in part. At a meeting in Brussels, and after five years of negotiations, representatives of the Ukrainian and European Union negotiating delegations initialed the 170-page political part of the Association Agreement.[254] In addition to the political provisions, the Association Agreement contains a 180-page economic part and 1,350 pages of appendices. These cover all trade-related issues, regulating questions of competition, customs, energy, intellectual property, public procurement, services, and sustainable development. Though these provisions have yet to be initialed, they will undoubtedly improve Ukraine's investment climate and help develop business cooperation.

The next step in the association process will be for the two parties to sign the Association Agreement and submit it to the European Parliament and each of the parliaments of the 27 member states for ratification. No timetable has been set for the process of ratifying the accord, and according to the European Union, progress "will be

---

[253]Ibid.

[254]Kyiv Post, "EU Sets Conditions on Closer Ties with Ukraine," March 30, 2011, http://www.kyivpost.com/news/nation/detail/125252/ (accessed April 1, 2012); Europa Press Releases, Rapid, "European Union and Ukrainian Negotiators initial Association Agreement, including Deep and Comprehensive Free Trade Area," March 30, 2012, MEMO/12/238, http://europa.eu/rapid/pressReleasesAction.do?reference=MEMO/12/238 &type =HTML (accessed April 1, 2012). Negotiations leading to the Association Agreement between Ukraine and the European Union started on March 5, 2007, and included 21 rounds of negotiations. The negotiating process was finalized on December 19, 2011.

very much influenced by the political situation in Ukraine."[255] Although the Association Agreement will establish closer political, economic, cultural, and social ties between the European Union and Ukraine, and promote the rule of law, democracy, and human rights in Ukraine, officials for the European Union have said that it would take effect only if the political climate in Kyiv became more "European."[256] This raises some doubt about the future of the Association Agreement, particularly in light of concerns expressed in recent months about the independence of Ukraine's judiciary, the arrest of opposition leaders, and the perceived absence of free and fair elections.[257] Gunther Krichbaum, Germany's Chairman of the Committee on the Affairs of the European Union, said as much during an interview following the initialing of the Association Agreement.

> There's no doubt that relations between Ukraine and the European Union will intensify. But as for the initialing of the Association Agreement, we're speaking about a technical process of the completion of work on the document. The issue is not over . . . The European Union has certain standards and values. Ukraine claims about its aspiration to support these values. We're speaking about the principles of a legal state, democracy, respect for freedom of speech and many

---

[255]Ibid. Once an agreement is reached, it will need to be ratified by the European Parliament and Ukraine's *Verkhovna Rada*. Bureaucratic procedures, such as translating the 1,700 page agreement into all 23 official languages of the European Union will take months, and could lead to a gap of up to or in excess of a year between the signing of the agreement and its entry into force. Ukrainian Foreign Minister Kostiantyn Gryshchenko expressed hope that the Association Agreement will be signed within the next twelve months. See, Kyiv Post, "Gryshchenko: Kyiv Hopes to Sign Association Agreement with EU within 12 Months," March 30, 2012, http://www.kyivpost.com/news/nation/detail/125242/ (accessed April 1, 2012).

[256]Ibid.

[257]Ibid. A senior European Union official states that the "personal fate of Yulia Tymoshenko is the tip of the iceberg . . . It's about the impartiality of the judicial process in general . . . We expect the adoption of European values."

other [values]. We'd like to see certain efforts and serious progress, support for civil society. We can't see all this at the moment, unfortunately.[258]

Signing the Association Agreement and establishing a Deep and Comprehensive Free Trade Area will undoubtedly further strengthen Ukraine's economic integration and regulatory convergence with the European Union. Yet the future of the Association Agreement, as well as Ukraine's broader aspirations of further integration with the European Union, is a matter of political will for the Ukrainian government.

At the 15th Ukraine-European Union Summit in Kyiv in mid-December 2011, European Commission President José Manuel Barroso confirmed this when he declared that the "key to strengthen our relationship is in the hands of the Ukrainian authorities."[259] Indeed, whether Ukraine is hastening the process of integration depends on political developments in Ukraine; according to Ina Kirsch, Head of the European Centre for Modern Ukraine in Brussels: it cannot be solved simply by espousing "beautiful words about the importance of Ukraine's European integration process."[260] Kirsch's words uncomfortably recall the early criticisms of James Sherr and Kataryna Wolczuk, both of whom faulted Ukraine for not adopting domestic institutional reforms

---

[258]Kyiv Post, "Bundestag Not Planning to Ratify Ukraine-EU Association Agreement yet," March 31, 2012, http://www.kyivpost.com/news/nation/detail/125264/ (accessed April 1, 2012). "When we speak about values of the European Union, they should not be just shared, they should guide. Ukraine is implementing reforms not for Germany or the European Union, but for the sake of its citizens. There is much work to be done here."

[259]Press TV, "Ukraine's EU membership Put on Hold," December 20, 2011, http://presstv.com/detail/216824.html (accessed April 1, 2012).

[260]Kyiv Post, "Future of the Association Agreement Depends on Specific Actions, Says European Expert," March 31, 2012, http://www.kyivpost.com/news/nation/detail/ 125269/ (accessed April 1, 2012). "Intensive discussions and concrete measures are now necessary to cement the foundation of this process and to make it truly irreversible."

or exercising strong political initiative to fully embrace the process of Europeanization. While there is evidence that Ukraine's current political leadership recognizes the importance of adopting concrete measures, particularly in the area of democratic reforms, further guaranteeing the process of European integration, there is the question of whether Ukraine faces sufficient pressures from within its own society as well as from the European Union. In order for Ukraine to continue Europeanizing and to adopt required judicial reforms, there needs to be increasing pressure from Ukrainians who support further integration as well as from the rule-setting agency itself--the European Union.

During a March 30 telephone conversation with Polish President Bronisław Komorowski, President Yanukovych extended an invitation to international observers from Poland and other European countries to monitor Ukraine's parliamentary elections scheduled for October 28, 2012.[261] Indeed, the signing of the Association Agreement may very well be subject to Ukraine's guaranteeing free and democratic procedures during its October parliamentary elections. Rebecca Harm, leader of the Greens in the European Parliament has publicly stated that Ukraine's elections will be closely scrutinized and that signing the Association Agreement is contingent upon Ukraine making "substantial efforts to guarantee political plurality and to address major human rights concerns."[262] Because of its superior bargaining position, the European Union may simply withhold the signing and eventual ratification of the Association Agreement

---

[261]Kyiv Post, "Ukrainian, Polish Presidents Hail Initialing of Association Agreement between Ukraine and EU," March 31, 2012, http://www.kyivpost.com/ news/nation/detail/ 125271/ (accessed April 1, 2012).

[262]Kyiv Post, "European Greens: No Signing of Association Agreement until Ukraine Reforming," March 30, 2012, http://www.kyivpost.com/news/nation/detail/ 125239/ (accessed April 1, 2012).

dependent on Ukraine successfully adopting reforms within its judiciary and taking further steps to guarantee democracy under the rule of law.

At the time of Ukraine's Orange Revolution, opposition leader Viktor Yushchenko hinted that he would press the European Union for deeper ties and described a four-point plan: acknowledgment of Ukraine as a market economy, entry in the World Trade Organization, associate membership in the European Union, and, finally, full membership.[263] Yushchenko achieved half of his goals. During his presidency, Yushchenko witnessed Ukraine's accession to the World Trade Organization, and on June 16, 2009, the European Union and Ukraine adopted an Association Agenda which has since led to finalization of the Association Agreement and Deep and Comprehensive Free Trade Area. Arguably Ukraine is progressing along the path of establishing itself as a market economy. Membership in the European Union remains however a (not too) distant goal for Ukraine's European aspirations. As a result of Ukraine's successful efforts at undergoing the process of Europeanization in the areas of economic integration and energy cooperation, membership aspirations are no longer an uncertain or elusive goal for Ukraine.

Economic and political integration with the European Union remain popular, long-term goals for Ukrainians and Ukraine's business elites would undoubtedly welcome better access to European export markets. The European Union, however, needs to leverage its appeal to spur Ukraine towards furthering its efforts at Europeanization. Assisted by the European Union, Ukraine must make its gas sector more efficient and

---

[263]Yushchenko served as Ukraine's 3rd president from January 3, 2005 until February 25, 2010.

transparent as such reforms would reduce energy security threats for the European Union by reducing the likelihood of future quarrels between Russia and Ukraine. Similarly, the European Union can encourage Ukraine along the path of judicial and democratic reform by making further progress on the Association Agreement and the Deep and Comprehensive Free Trade Area contingent upon free and democratic parliamentary elections scheduled for October 2012. Moreover, the European Union's criticism of the trial and conviction of Yulia Tymoshenko should persuade Ukraine of the necessity for judicial reforms aimed at ensuring Ukraine's commitment to a fair, transparent and impartial legal process.

European integration remains the strategic aim of Ukraine, but if it is to have a future in Europe, Ukraine must embrace increased efforts at Europeanization within its judicial and political institutions comparable to what it has achieved in its economic and energy sectors. Absent strong incentives from the European Union to adopt concrete judicial reforms, Ukraine's record of Europeanization, though much more promising compared to what it had been before the Orange Revolution, remains ultimately mixed.

APPENDIX A

Overview of European Union-Ukraine Relations

Ukraine is the largest country located entirely in Europe, and following the 2004/2007 Eastern enlargement, it now borders four member states of the European Union: Poland, Slovakia, Hungary and Romania. It is one of the most densely populated countries in Europe, and ranks fifth after Germany, Italy, Great Britain, and France with a total population of 45.6 million.[264] Despite the fact that its oil and natural gas reserves have been largely exhausted, Ukraine remains relatively rich in natural resources, particularly in mineral deposits.[265] Ukraine possesses 30 percent of the world's richest black soil and there is great potential for its agricultural industry. In 2008, Ukraine was the European Union's 17th largest trading partner and 14th largest export market. Conversely, the European Union was Ukraine's largest trading partner, with 27.1 percent of its total exports and 33.7 percent of imports in 2008.[266]

---

[264]As of October 1, 2011, Ukraine's population total is 45,665,281. See, State Statistics Service of Ukraine, http://www.ukrstat.gov.ua (accessed March 15, 2012).

[265]Ukraine is rich in natural resources: coal, iron ore, manganese, nickel and uranium, and others. Its reserves of sulfur are the largest in the world, and its reserves of mercury ore are the second largest. More than 5 percent of world reserves of iron ore are concentrated in Ukraine. See, Ministry of Foreign Affairs of Ukraine, http://www.mfa. gov.ua (accessed March 15, 2012).

[266]European Union-Ukraine trade reached 39.5 billion euro in 2008, an increase from 34.8 billion euro in 2007, and has been growing steadily in recent years. Agricultural products, energy, chemicals, iron and steel are main exports from Ukraine to the European Union. Imports from the European Union to Ukraine include machinery, transport equipment, chemicals, textiles and clothing, and agricultural products. See, "EU-Ukraine bilateral trade," Delegation of the European Union to Ukraine, European Union External Action Service, http://eeas.europa.eu/delegations/ukraine/eu_ukraine/ trade_relation/bilateral_trade/index_en.htm (accessed March 15, 2012). For current information on Ukraine's trade with the European Union, see, *Ukraine: EU Bilateral*

As early as 1993, the European Union opened a structured political dialogue with Ukraine which led to the signing of a Partnership and Cooperation Agreement on June 14, 1994. The strategic objectives of the Partnership and Cooperation Agreement committed the European Union and Ukraine to establishing a partnership providing for close political and mutually beneficial trade and investment relations together with economic, social, financial, civil, scientific, technological and cultural cooperation. The partnership, in particular, established a legal framework based on the respect of democratic principles and human rights and set forth the political, economic and trade relationship between the European Union and Ukraine.[267]

Starting in the mid-1990s, the European Union opened membership negotiations with Ukraine's neighbours in Central and Eastern Europe, including Poland, Slovakia and Hungary. It seemed to many Ukrainians, who consider themselves Europeans, that they too should have been part of the membership ngotiations with the European Union. This was the view of not only the Ukrainian elite, whose business ties with Western Europe were growing, but also of the general populace who desired to attain the living standards of the European Union members. In November 1995, the Council of Europe admitted Ukraine and by early 1996, Ukraine's President, Leonid Kuchma made several speeches explicitly emphasizing Ukraine's "European Choice." At a forum in Helsinki in February, Kuchma remarked that "[t]he cradle of Ukrainian culture is European Christian

---

Trade and Trade with the World, January 10, 2012, http://trade.ec.europa.eu/doclib/docs/ 2006/september/tradoc_113459.pdf (accessed March 15, 2012).

[267]See, European Commission, *European Neighbourhood and Partnership Instrument, Ukraine, Country Strategy Paper, 2007-2013*, http://ec.europa.eu/world/enp/ pdf/country/enpi_csp_ukraine_en.pdf (accessed March 15, 2012).

civilization. That is why our home is, above all, Europe."[268] In the fall of 1997, a European and Transatlantic Integration Administration was created within the Ukrainian Ministry of Foreign Affairs that included a European Union Department and shortly thereafter, a top-ranking diplomat was named to the newly created post of representative to the European Communities.[269] In addition, the National Agency of Ukraine for Reconstruction and Development became the National Agency of Ukraine for Development and European Integration. This was soon followed in June 1998--three months after the Partnership and Cooperation Agreement came into force--with Kuchma issuing a decree approving Ukraine's "Strategy of Integration into the European Union" which stated, in part, that the "national interests of Ukraine require identification of Ukraine as an influential European country, full-fledged European Union member."[270] The "Strategy" outlined the principal requirements of the process of European integration and included approximation of Ukrainian legislation to European Union legislation, political consolidation and the strengthening of democracy, economic integration and the

---

[268]*"Ukraina i maibutnye Yevropy:Vystup Prezydenta L.D. Kuchmy u tovarystvi im. Paasiivi* (m. Hel'sinki, Finlandiya) 8 lyutoho 1996 roku," *Polityka i chas* 3 (1996), 4, cited in Roman Solchanyk, *Ukraine and Russia: the post-Soviet Transition* (Lanham, MD: Rowan & Littlefield, 2001), 92. Solchanyk cites Kuchma's April 1996 address before the session of the Parliamentary Assembly of the Council of Europe in Strasbourg where he reaffirmed Ukraine's strategic goal of full membership in the European Union.

[269]Solchanyk, *Ukraine and Russia: the post-Soviet Transition*, 92.

[270]Kataryna Wolczuk, Integration without Europeanisation: Ukraine and Its Policy Towards the European Union, European Union Institute Working papers, RSCAS No. 2004/15 (Florence, Italy: Robert Schuman Centre for Advanced Studies, 2004), 6, http://www.eui.eu/RSCAS/ WP-Texts/04_15.pdf (accessed March 15, 2012). Wolczuk outlines the "Strategy" and its nine "Main Directions" foremost of which are the adaptation of the legislation of Ukraine to the *acquis communautaire* and protection of human rights.

development of trade, and cooperation in environmental protection and the field of justice and home affairs. Moreover, the "Strategy" set out the main priorities for state executive bodies for the period up to 2007, when Ukraine was expected to have met the conditions for full European Union membership.[271]

The "Strategy" envisaged "comprehensive integration of Ukraine into the European political, legal, economic, information and cultural environment" and "identification of the European Union policy towards Ukraine, its separation from the European Union policy towards Russia, and support of the European countries and the world community of the strategy of integration of Ukraine with the European Union."[272] The European Union appears to have largely ignored Ukraine's integration initiative, however, indicating at the time that Ukraine needed to first meet its obligations under the Partnership and Cooperation Agreement. In her study on Ukraine-European Union relations, Inna Pidluska comments that by the end of 1999, "Ukraine had failed to meet 22 provisions of the Partnership and Cooperation Agreement and was too far from meeting the requirements for joining the World Trade Organization to proceed to the creation of a free trade area with the European Union."[273] During the Kuchma presidency the European Union refused even to entertain the idea of Ukraine entering the Union, with Germany and France especially reluctant to irritate Russia.[274] In support of its

---

[271]Inna Pidluska, *Ukraine-EU Relations: Enlargement and Integration*, International Policy Fellowships, http://www.policy.hu/pidluska/EU-Ukraine.html (accessed March 15, 2012).

[272]Ibid.

[273]Ibid.

position, the European Commission argued that substantial economic and political

reforms were needed before any discussion of membership could occur.[275]

In his November 30, 1999 inaugural speech, President Kuchma announced:

"Reaffirming our European choice, we define joining the European Union as our strategic

goal."[276] The "Strategy of Integration into the European Union" was developed into an

ambitious "Programme of Integration of Ukraine to the European Union," and introduced

by presidential decree on September 14, 2000. A number of decrees and resolutions were

adopted to facilitate approximation of Ukrainian legislation to that of the European

Union, and a substantial volume of reports emerged describing the technical assistance

and advice provided to Ukraine. The practical result was limited however, due to the lack

of adequate institutions within Ukraine capable of producing the desired change.[277]

Although Ukraine remained rather slow in implementing the terms of the

Partnership and Cooperation Agreement, the European Union recognized its aspirations

for membership when the European Parliament issued its "Resolution on the Common

---

[274]Orest Subtelny, *Ukraine: A History*, 4th ed. (Toronto: University of Toronto Press, 2009), 645. The French population has generally been hostile towards enlargement ever since the question became topical after the fall of the Berlin Wall. According to a 2007 Eurobarometer poll, just 32 percent of respondents in France support the Union's future enlargement, against a European Union average of 46 percent. See, Toby Vogel, "France's Enlargement Pains," EuropeaeanVoice.com, June 19, 2008, http://www. europeanvoice. com/article/imported/france-s-enlargement-pains/61318.aspx (accessed March 15, 2012).

[275]Ibid., 644.

[276]Pidluska, *Ukraine-EU Relations: Enlargement and Integration.*

[277]Ibid. Pidluska comments that at the end of 1999, only about 400 out of 10,000 pieces of Ukrainian legislation actually met European standards.

Strategy of the European Union on Ukraine" on March 15, 2001.[278] The opening

paragraph of the "Resolution" acknowledged Ukraine's "strong ambition to deepen its

relations to the European Union" and to the then candidate countries of Central and

Eastern Europe, but then proceeded to outline a number of areas in which Ukraine needed

to undertake serious reform measures. Paragraph 11 of the "Resolution" criticized the

recent 1999 parliamentary and presidential elections as not abiding by "international

standards for democratic elections" and questioned the independence of Ukraine's media

for "not exercising their proper role in a democratic society."[279] The "Resolution"

congratulated Ukraine on the abolition of the death penalty in their criminal code, but

criticized Ukraine for lacking "democratically acceptable elections and the creation of an

independent judiciary, a professional and efficient administration and media free from all

interference."[280] Despite its aspirations of membership in the European Union at the turn

of the millennium, Ukraine was still very far from adopting the requisite legal and

institutional reforms. This was also during the same period when many of Ukraine's

Central and East European neighbours were succeeding in their efforts at

Europeanization.

---

[278]European Parliament Resolution on the Common Strategy of the European Union on Ukraine (C5-0208/2000-2000/2116(COS)), http://www.europarl.europa.eu (accessed March 15, 2012).

[279]Ibid., paragraph 11.

[280]Ibid., paragraphs 16 and 12. Paragraph 13 of the Resolution further criticized Ukraine for not adopting the "necessary legal and operational measures to combat discrimination based on sex, racial or ethnic origin, religion or belief, disability, age or sexual orientation, as well as discrimination in the field of employment."

The European Commission adopted a "Ukraine Country Strategy Paper" on December 27, 2001, outlining the strategic framework within which the European Union would provide technical assistance to Ukraine for trade liberalization and wide-ranging cooperation for the period 2002-2006.[281] The "Strategy Paper" placed priority of assistance on "strengthening democratic and civic institutions, particularly independent mass media, as well as the judiciary and public administration."[282] Acknowledging that in 2000 and 2001, Ukraine "initiated several important legal, judicial, institutional, social and economic reforms," it stressed the urgent need for Ukraine "to sustain economic growth through structural reforms, particularly in the energy and agricultural sectors" and "to establish a legal framework conducive to investment."[283] The areas highlighted in the summary of the "Strategy Paper" include economic, legal and energy reforms, and are the three principal areas of research that this present study addresses.[284]

Ukraine's efforts at undergoing Europeanization may be an open question, but on May 1, 2004, eight post-communist Central and Eastern European countries successfully joined the European Union in the largest single enlargement in terms of people and number of countries. The European Union firmly positioned Ukraine among the "post-

---

[281]European Commission, "Ukraine Country Strategy Paper 2002-2006," http://www.eeas.europa.eu/ukraine/csp/02_06_en.pdf (accessed March 15, 2012).

[282]Ibid., 1.

[283]Ibid. "The energy sector requires particular attention, as Ukraine is an important transit country for energy supplies from Russia and is heavily dependent on oil and gas imports, largely due to very inefficient energy use."

[284]The European Commission has since issued a "European Neighbourhood and Partnership Instrument, Ukraine Country Strategy Paper, 2006-2013." See, http://ec. europa.eu/world/enp/pdf/country/ enpi_csp_ukraine_en.pdf (accessed March 15, 2012).

communist borderline countries which had less favorable initial (political and economic) conditions" compared with other Central and Eastern European countries and "where domestic reforms lagged during the initial years of post-communist transition."[285] At this point, it is of little value to conjecture why the European Union did not engage Ukraine more closely as it did the other countries of Central and Eastern Europe during the 1990s, or offer membership incentives which might have fostered domestic reforms encouraging Ukraine to commit itself more boldly to the process of Europeanization. While it may be unfair to criticize the European Union for failing to assert itself more forcefully in Ukraine's affairs during the first decade of its transition from communism, mention must be made of the European Union's short-sightedness for not seizing the opportunity to support political and judicial reform that presented itself in the months following Ukraine's Orange Revolution of 2004.[286]

The series of protests and political demonstrations that marked Ukraine's Orange Revolution from November 2004 to January 2005, were the result of a disputed November 21 run-off vote between leading presidential candidates Viktor Yushchenko and Viktor Yanukovych. The 2004 Ukrainian presidential election was marred by massive corruption, voter intimidation and direct electoral fraud. Kyiv served as the focal point of the movement's campaign of civil resistance. Ukraine's Supreme Court ordered a

---

[285]Inna Melnykovska, "Ukraine: Europeanization from abroad or inside? Chance and Challenge for the European Union," paper prepared for the European Community Study Association-Canada 2008 Biennial Conference, "The Maturing European Union" Edmonton, Alberta, September 25-27, 2008, 2. See, http://web.uvic.ca/ecsac/biennial 2008/Conference%20Program_files/Melnykovska.pdf (accessed March 15, 2012).

[286]Grzegorz Gromadzki, *et al.*, *Will the Orange Revolution bear fruit? EU– Ukraine relations in 2005 and the beginning of 2006* (Warsaw: Stefan Batory Foundation, 2005), http://www.batory.org.pl/ doc/orange.pdf (accessed March 15, 2012).

revote for December 26, 2004, and under intense scrutiny by domestic and international observers, the second run-off was declared to be fair and free.[287] Carried out "by a coalition of diversified domestic forces" the Orange Revolution has been criticized for "failing to build any consistent and unified vision of the future" for Ukraine.[288] Following Yushchenko's inauguration on January 23, 2005, the leaders of Ukraine's opposition were unable to consolidate power and the Orange Revolution came to an abrupt end. The European Union supported the Orange Revolution by criticizing the electoral fraud during the elections and encouraging Ukraine to adopt changes to its 1994 Constitution. On the other hand, the European Union did not seize the advantages offered by the Orange Revolution and offered no incentives to Ukraine to consolidate the domestic forces at work which might have spurred the process of Europeanization.[289] Instead of the prospect of membership, the European Union offered Ukraine its European Neighbour-hood Policy.

The European Security Strategy of 2003 aspired to create "a world seen as offering justice and opportunity for everyone" and affirmed the European Union's

---

[287]Subtelny, *A History of Ukraine*, 636-643. Yushchenko declared victory after having received about 52 percent of the vote, compared to Yanukovych's 44 percent. Yushchenko's inauguration on January 23, 2005 in Kyiv signaled the end of the Orange Revolution. See, *Центральна Виборча Комісія України* (Central Election Commission of Ukraine), http://www.cvk.gov.ua/ pls/vp2004/wp0011 (accessed March 15, 2012).

[288]Melnykovska, "Ukraine: Europeanization from abroad or inside?," 2.

[289]Despite the European Union's lack of engagement during the Orange Revolution, Ukraine succeeded in bringing about some European Union-style democratic reforms. Significantly, the Ukrainian constitution was changed to shift powers from the presidency to the parliament. On October 1, 2010, however, the Constitutional Court of Ukraine overturned the 2004 amendments. See, Kyiv Post, "Update: Return to 1996 Constitution strengthens president, raises legal questions," October 1, 2010, http://www.kyivpost.com/news/politics/detail/84619/ (accessed March 15, 2012).

intention to work proactively towards this end.[290] The following year, the European

Commission developed the European Neighbourhood Policy aimed at avoiding new

dividing lines between the recently enlarged European Union and 16 of its closest

neighbours.[291] It offered a vision involving "a ring of countries, sharing the European

Union's fundamental values and objectives, drawn into an increasingly close relationship,

going beyond co-operation to involve a significant measure of economic and political

integration."[292] Modeled on the success of the European Union's Eastern enlargement,

the European Neighbourhood Policy sought "to define an alternative incentive for

domestic reform in neighbouring countries, referred to as having 'a stake in the internal

market.'"[293] A March 2003 Communication from the Commission to the Council and the

---

[290]European Council, "A Secure Europe in a Better World: European Security Strategy," December 12, 2003, 10, http://www.consilium.europa.eu/uedocs/cmsUpload/78367.pdf (accessed March 15, 2012).

[291]In addition to Ukraine, the European Neighbourhood Policy includes partner states Algeria, Armenia, Azerbaijan, Belarus, Egypt, Georgia, Israel, Jordan, Lebanon, Libya, Moldova, Morocco, Occupied Palestinian Territory, Syria and Tunisia. See, European Commission, European Neighbourhood Policy, http://ec.europa.eu/world/enp/index_en.htm (March 15, 2012).

[292]European Commission, "European Neighbourhood Policy Strategy Paper," May 12, 2004, COM(2004), 373 final, http://ec.europa.eu/world/enp/pdf/strategy/strategy_paper_en.pdf (accessed March 15, 2012). For comprehensive analyses of the European Neighbourhood Policy, see generally, Esther Barbé and Elisabeth Johansson-Nogués, "The EU as a Modest 'Force for Good': the European Neighbourhood Policy," *International Affairs* 84, no. 1(January 2008): 81-96 and Amichai Magen, "The Shadow of Enlargement: Can the European Neighbourhood Policy Achieve Compliance?" *The Columbia Journal of European Law* 12, no. 2 (Spring 2006): 383-427.

[293]Gwendolyn Sasse, "The European Neighbourhood Policy: Conditionality Revisited for the EU's Eastern Neighbours," *Europe-Asia Studies* 60, no. 2 (2008): 295-316.

European Parliament, provided an initial outline of the intended purpose of the European

Neighbourhood Policy:

> In return for concrete progress demonstrating shared values and effective
> implementation of political, economic and institutional reforms, including in
> aligning legislation with the *acquis*, the EU's neighbourhood should benefit from
> the prospect of closer economic integration with the European Union. To this end,
> Russia, the countries of the Western NIS and the Southern Mediterranean should
> be offered the prospect of a stake in the European Union's Internal Market and
> further integration and liberalisation to promote the free movement of persons,
> goods, services and capital (four freedoms).[294]

The European Neighbourhood Policy is a bilateral policy between the European Union

and each partner country. It encourages non-member states to Europeanize--to adopt

"political, economic and institutional reforms" consistent with the *acquis*

communautaire--but does so without the explicit promise of membership within the

European Union. Despite its initial aspirations of furthering "integration and

liberalization," however, the European Neighbourhood Policy has been criticized for

poorly defining the elements of conditionality and for lacking clear incentive and

enforcement structures.[295] Initially, Ukraine viewed the European Neighbourhood Policy

"with coolness and distrust" claiming that it failed to "appreciate Ukraine's European

---

[294]European Commission, "Communication from the Commission to the Council and the European Parliament, 'Wider Europe—Neighbourhood: A New Framework for Relations with our Eastern and Southern Neighbours,'" March 11, 2003, COM(2003), 104 final. The "countries of the Western NIS" refer to Belarus, Moldova and Ukraine.

[295]See, Sasse, "The European Neighbourhood Policy." See also, Claire Gordon and Gwendolyn Sasse, *The European Neighbourhood Policy: Effective Instrument for Conflict Management and Democratic Change in the Union's Eastern Neighbourhood?* (Bolzano, Italy: European Academy, 2008), www.eurac.edu (accessed March 15, 2012). The European Commission compiled a comprehensive listing of publicly available background research on the European Neighbourhood Policy. The Commission's most recent 17-page listing includes reports and articles through December 7, 2010. See, http://ec.europa.eu/world/enp/pdf/background_material.pdf (accessed March 15, 2012).

identity or its ambitions to join the European Union and [treated] it on the same basis as countries of North Africa."[296]

Subsequent European Union regional and multilateral co-operation initiatives include the Union for the Mediterranean created in July 2008[297] and its counterpart the Eastern Partnership, launched in Prague on May 7, 2009.[298] The Warsaw-based Polish Institute of International Affairs published an Opening Report on the Eastern Partnership in May 2009, and remarked that Ukraine "greeted positively" the Eastern Partnership "in large measure precisely because it singles out the 'European neighbours of the European Union'."[299] Earlier, however, on December 3, 2008, when the European Commission announced the Eastern Partnership, the Ukrainian Ministry of Foreign Affairs declared that Ukraine would only cooperate if the program did not constitute an alternative to future European Union membership, and that it would serve to bring Ukraine closer to

---

[296]Beata Wojna and Mateusz Gniazdowski, eds., *Eastern Partnership: the Opening Report* (Warsaw: The International Institute of International Affairs, 2009), 67.

[297]See, Union for the Mediterranean, http://www.ufmsecretariat.org (accessed March 15, 2012).

[298]The foreign minister of Poland with assistance from Sweden presented the initial proposal at the European Union's General Affairs and External Relations Council in Brussels on May 26, 2008. See, Renata Goldirova, "'Eastern Partnership'could lead to enlargement, Poland says," May 27, 2008, EUObserver.com, http://euobserver.com/ 24/26211 (accessed March 15, 2012). The Eastern Partnership consists of all 27 member states of the European Union and six post-Soviet states: Armenia, Azerbaijan, Belarus, Georgia, Republic of Moldova and Ukraine. See, European Union External Action Service, Eastern Partnership, http://eeas.europa.eu/eastern/index_ en.htm (accessed March 15, 2012). See also, Eastern Partnership Community, http://www.eastern partnership.org/ (accessed March 15, 2012).

[299]Wojna and Gniazdowski, eds., *Eastern Partnership: the Opening Report*, 67.

that goal.[300] The concern voiced by the Ukrainian Ministry of Foreign Affairs reflects a

common distrust among Ukrainians who support European Union membership. The

editors of the Opening Report commented that "[g]enerally speaking, Ukraine cannot get

rid of a certain distrust with regard to this initiative out of fear that some Western

European politicians see the Eastern Partnership not as a stage on the way to European

Union membership, but as a substitute for it."[301]

---

[300]Ibid., 68. See generally, Kataryna Wolczuk, "Perceptions of, and Attitudes towards, the Eastern Partnership amongst the Partner Countries' Political Elites," *Eastern Partnership Review*, No. 5 (Tallinn: Estonian Centre of Eastern Partnership, December 2011), www.eceap.edu/ (accessed March 15, 2012).

[301]Ibid. See also, Taras Kuzio, "Ukraine's Relations with the West: Disinterest, Partnership, Disillusionment," *European Security* 12, no. 2 (Summer 2003): 21-44.

BIBLIOGRAPHY

Primary Sources

Negotiations on the European Union-Ukraine Association Agreement

4th Joint Progress Report, Negotiations on the EU-Ukraine Association Agreement, November 2010.

3rd Joint Progress Report, Negotiations on the EU-Ukraine Association Agreement, November 2009.

2nd Joint Progress Report, Negotiations on the New Enhanced Agreement, September 2008.

1st Joint Progress Report, Negotiations on the New Enhanced Agreement, September 2007.

European Union-Ukraine Association Agenda

EU-Ukraine Association Agenda Priorities for Action 2011-12, May 2011.

EU-Ukraine Association Agenda, May 2011.

Joint Report Regarding Progress in Implementation of the Joint Committee at Senior Official Level of the EU-Ukraine Association Agenda to the EU-Ukraine Cooperation Council, June 2010.

EU-Ukraine Association Agenda Priorities for Action 2010, January 2010.

EU-Ukraine Association Agenda, November 2009.

European Neighbourhood Policy Progress Reports Ukraine

Implementation of the ENP in 2011: Country Report Ukraine, May 2012.

Implementation of the ENP in 2010: Country Report Ukraine, May 2011.

European Neighbourhood Policy: Progress Report 2009, May 2010.

European Neighbourhood Policy: Progress Report 2008, April 2009.

Implementation of the ENP in 2007: Progress Report Ukraine, April 2008.

Strengthening the ENP: ENP Progress Report Ukraine, December 2006.

European Neighbourhood Policy Country Report Ukraine, May 2004.

Memorandum of Understanding on Co-operation in the Field of Energy
between the European Union and Ukraine

*6th Joint EU-Ukraine Report, Implementation of the EU-Ukraine Memorandum of
Understanding on Energy Co-operation during 2011*, March 2012.

*5th Joint Progress Report on the Implementation of the EU-Ukraine Memorandum of
Understanding on Energy Co-operation during 2010*, November 2010.

*4th Joint Progress Report on the Implementation of the EU-Ukraine Memorandum of
Understanding on Energy Co-operation during 2009*, December 2009.

*Joint Declaration: Joint EU-Ukrainian Investment Conference on the Modernisation of
Ukraine's Gas Transit System*, March 2009.

*3rd Joint Progress Report on the Implementation of the EU-Ukraine Memorandum of
Understanding on Energy Co-operation during 2008*, August 2008.

*2nd Joint Progress Report on the Implementation of the EU-Ukraine Memorandum of
Understanding on Energy Co-operation during 2007*, September 2007.

*1st Joint Progress Report on the Implementation of the EU-Ukraine Memorandum of
Understanding on Energy Co-operation during 2006*, October 2006.

*Memorandum of Understanding on Co-operation in the Field of Energy between the
European Union and Ukraine*, December 2005.

Agreement between the European Atomic Energy Community and the Cabinet of
Ministers of Ukraine for Co-operation in the Peaceful Uses of Nuclear Energy

*Agreement between the European Atomic Energy Community and the Cabinet of
Ministers of Ukraine for Co-operation in the Peaceful Uses of Nuclear Energy*,
April 2005.

European Union-Ukraine Action Plan

Joint Evaluation Report EU-Ukraine Action Plan, March 2008.

European Union-Ukraine Action Plan, February 2005.

European Union-Ukraine Partnership and Cooperation Agreement

EU-Ukraine Partnership and Cooperation Agreement, January 1998.

Books

Bache, Ian, and Stephen George. *Politics in the European Union.* 3rd ed. Oxford: Oxford University Press, 2011.

Baldwin, Richard, and Charles Wyplosz. *The Economics of European Integration.* 3rd ed. London: McGraw Hill Education, 2009.

Bankowski, Zenon, and Andrew Scott, eds. *The European Union and Its Order: The Legal Theory of European Integration.* Oxford: Blackwell, 2000.

Center for Peace, Conversion and Foreign Policy of Ukraine. *European Integration of Ukraine as Viewed by Top Ukrainian Politicians, Businessmen and Society Leaders.* Warsaw: Center for Peace, Conversion and Foreign Policy of Ukraine, 2003.

Checkel, Jeffrey T., and Peter J. Katzenstein, eds. *European Identity.* Contemporary European Politics. Cambridge: Cambridge University, 2009.

Cowles, Maria Green, James Caporaso and Thomas Risse, eds. *Transforming Europe: Europeanization and Domestic Change.* Ithaca: Cornell University, 2001.

D'Anieri, Paul, ed. *Orange Revolution and Aftermath: Mobilization, Apathy, and the State in Ukraine.* Baltimore, MD: Johns Hopkins University Press, 2010.

Dabrowski, Marek, and Svitlana Taran. *The Free Trade Agreement Between the EU and Ukraine: Conceptual Background, Economic Context and Potential Impact.* Brussels: European Parliament, Directorate-General for External Policies, October 2011.

Dinan, Desmond. *Ever Closer Union: An Introduction to EuropeanIintegration*, 4th ed. Boulder, CO: Lynne Rienner, 2010.

———. ed. *Origins and Evolution of the European Union.* The New European Union Series. Oxford: Oxford University Press, 2006.

Emerson, Michael, comp. *The Prospect of Deep Free Trade between the European Union and Ukraine.* Brussels: Centre For European Policy Studies, 2006.

Favell, Adrian, and Virginie Guiraudon. *Sociology of the European Union.* New York: Palgrave Macmillan, 2011.

Febbrajo, Alberto, and Wojciech Sadurski, eds. *Central and Eastern Europe after Transition: Towards a New Socio-legal Semantics.* Surrey: Ashgate, 2010.

Fligstein, Neil. *Euroclash: The EU, European Identity, and the Future of Europe.* Oxford: Oxford University, 2009.

Fontaine, Pascal. *New Idea for Europe: the Shuman Declaration--1950-2000*, 2nd ed. Luxembourg: Office for Official Publications of the European Communities, 2000.

Gazizullin, Ildar, and Larion Lozovyy. *Ukraine's Gas Market: Europeanization and the Russian Factor*, International Centre for Policy Studies. Kyiv: United States Agency for International Development, 2011.

Gilbert, Mark F. *Surpassing Realism: The Politics of European Integration Since 1945*. Lanham, MD: Rowman and Littlefield, 2003.

Graziano, P., and M. Vink, eds. *Europeanization: New Research Agendas*. Basingstoke: Palgrave Macmillan, 2007.

Haas, Ernst B. *The Uniting of Europe: Political, Social, and Economic Forces 1950-57*. Stanford, CA: Stanford University Press, 1958.

Haggard, Stephen, Marc A. Levy, Andrew Moravcsik, and Kalypso Nicolaïdis. "Integrating the Two Halves of Europe: Theories of Interests, Bargaining, and Institutions." In *After the Cold War: International Institutions and State Strategies in Europe 1989-1991*, edited by Robert O. Keohane, Joseph S. Nye, and Stanley Hoffmann, 173-195. Cambridge: Harvard University Press, 1993.

Henderson, Karen, ed. *Back to Europe: Central and Eastern Europe and the European Union*. London: University College of London, 1999.

Hughes, James, Gwendolyn Sasse and Claire Gordon. *Europeanization and Regionalization in the EU's Enlargement to Central & Eastern Europe: The Myth of Conditionality*. New York: Palgrave MacMillan, 2004.

Jacoby, Wade. *The Enlargement of the European Union and NATO: Ordering from the Menu in Central Europe*. Cambridge: Cambridge University, 2004.

Korosteleva, Elena, ed. *Eastern Partnership: A New Opportunity for the Neighbours?* London: Routledge, 2011.

Ladrech, Robert. *Europeanization and National Politics*. The European Union Series. New York: Palgrave, 2010.

Mayhew, Alan. *Recreating Europe: The European Union's Policy towards Central and Eastern Europe*. Cambridge: Cambridge University Press, 1998.

Maresceau, Marc, ed. *Enlarging the European Union: The relations between the EU and Central and Eastern Europe*. New York: Longman, 1997.

125

Moravcsik, Andrew. *The Choice for Europe: Social Purpose & State Power from Messina to Maastricht*. Cornell Studies in Political Economy, Ithaca: Cornell University Press, 1998.

O'Brennan, John, ed. *The Eastern Enlargement of the European Union*. New York: Routledge, 2006.

Pełczyńska-Nałęcz, Katarzyna. *Integration or Imitation? EU Policy towards its Eastern Neighbours*. Warsaw: Centre for Eastern Studies, 2011.

Radaelli, Claudio. "The Europeanization of Public Policy." In *The Politics of Europeanization*, edited by Kevin Featherstone and Claudio Radelli, 27-56. Oxford: Oxford University Press, 2003.

Risse, Thomas. *A Community of Europeans? Transnational Identities and Public Spheres* Ithaca: Cornell University, 2010.

Rosamond, Ben. *Theories of European Integration*. New York: Palgrave, 2000.

Sasse, Gwendolyn. "The ENP and the EU's Eastern Neighbous: Ukraine and Moldova as Test Cases." In *The European Neighbourhood Policy in Perspective: Context, Implementation and Impact*, edited by Richard G. Whitman and Stefan Wolff, 182-205. Palgrave Studies in European Union Politics. New York: Palgrave Macmillan, 2009.

Schimmelfennig, Frank, and Ulrich Sedelmeier, eds. *The Europeanization of Central and Eastern Europe*, Ithaca: Cornell University Press, 2005

———. eds., *The Politics of European Union Enlargement: Theoretical Approaches*. London: Routledge, 2005.

Sedelmeier, Ulrich. *Constructing the Path to Eastern Enlargement: The Uneven Policy Impact of EU Identity*. Manchester: Manchester University Press, 2005.

———. "Eastern Enlargement: Risk, Rationality, and Role-Compliance." In *Risks, Reforms, Resistance and Revival*, vol.5 of *The State of the European Union*, edited by Maria Green Cowles and Michael Smith, 164-185. Oxford: Oxford University Press, 2000.

Sherr, James. *Ukraine's New Time of Troubles*. Institut for Forsvarsstudier, ISO Info 6/1998. Oslo: Norwegian Institute for Defence Studies, 1998.

Shore, Cris. *Building Europe: The Cultural Politics of European Integration*. New York: Routledge, 2000.

Sushko, Oleksandr, Iulian Chifu, and Oazu Nantoi. *Russia-Ukraine 2009 Gas Crisis: Comparative view from Kyiv, Bucharest and Chisinau.* Kyiv: Institute for Euro-Atlantic Cooperation, 2010.

Skålnes, L. S. "Geopolitics and the Eastern Enlargement of the European Union." In *The Politics of European Union Enlargement: Theoretical Approaches*, edited by Frank Schimmelfennig and Ulrich Sedelmeier, 213-233. London: Routledge, 2005.

Snyder, Francis, ed. *The Europeanization of Law: The Legal Effects of European Integration.* Oxford: Hart Publishing, 2005.

Tatham, Allan F. *Enlargement of the European Union.* Kluwer European Law Collection 4. Netherlands: Kluwer Law International, 2009.

Trybus, Martin. *European Union Law and Defence Integration.* Oxford: Hart Publishing, 2005.

Valasek, Tomas. "Why Ukraine Matters to Europe." *Centre for European Reform Essays.* London: Centre for European Reform, 2008.

Weatherill, Stephen. *Law and Integration in the European Union.* Clarendon Law Series. Oxford: Clarendon Press, 1995.

Whitman, Richard G., and Stefan Wolff, eds. *The European Neighbourhood Policy in Perspective: Context, Implementation and Impact.* Palgrave Studies in European Union Politics. New York: Palgrave Macmillan, 2009.

Wiener, Antje, and Thomas Diez, eds. *European Integration Theory*, 2d. ed. Oxford: Oxford University Press, 2009.

Wolczuk, Kataryna "Integration without Europeanisation: Ukraine and its Policy towards the European Union," *European Union Institute Working Papers*, RSCAS No. 2004/15. Florence, Italy: Robert Schuman Centre for Advanced Studies, 2004.

Journal Articles

Barbé, Esther, and Elisabeth Johansson-Nogués. "The EU as a Modest 'Force for Good': the European Neighbourhood Policy." *International Affairs* 84, no. 1(January 2008): 81-96.

Baun, Michael, Jakub Dürr, Dan Marek, and Pavel Saradin. "The Europeanization of Czech Politics: The Political Parties and the EU Referendum." *Journal of Common Market Studies* 44, no. 2 (2006): 249-80.

Cirtautas, Arista Marie, and Frank Schimmelfennig. "Europeanisation Before and After Accession: Conditionality, Legacies and Compliance." *Europe-Asia Studies* 62, no. 3 (May 2010): 421-441.

Copsey, Nathaniel, and Alan Mayhew, eds., "European Neighbourhood Policy: the Case of Ukraine." *Sussex European Institute Seminar Papers Series*, no. 1 (January 2007).

Delcour, Laure. "Does the European Neighbourhood Policy Make a Difference? Policy Patterns and Reception in Ukraine and Russia." *European Political Economy Review*, Special Issue no. 7 (Summer 2007): 118-155.

Fierke, K. M., and A. Wiener. "Constructing Institutional Interests: EU and NATO Enlargement." *Journal of European Public* Policy 6, no. 5 (December 1999).

Grabbe, Heather. "European Union Conditionality and the Acquis Communautaire." *International Political Science Review* 23, no. 3 (July 2002): 249-268.

Knill, Christoph, and Dirk Lehmkuhl. "How Europe Matters: Different Mechanisms of Europeanization." *European Integration Online Papers* 3, no. 7 (1999).

Kovács,Melinda, and Olena Leipnik. "The Borders of Orientalism: "Europeanization" in Hungary and Ukraine." *Debatte* 16, no. 2 (August 2008): 151-169.

Kuzio, Taras. "Strident, Ambiguous and Duplicitous: Ukraine and the 2008 Russia-Georgia War." *Demokratizatsiya.* 17, no. 4 (Fall 2009): 350-372.

Kuszewska, Katarzyna. "The Challenges of Europeanization: on the Example of Poland--the New Member State of the EU." *E-Magazine.* http://www.cailaw.org/ academy/magazine/Europeanization-article.pdf (accessed March 18, 2012).

Larrabee, F. Stephen. "Russia, Ukraine, and Central Europe: The Return of Geopolitics." *Journal of International Affairs* 63, no. 2 (Spring/Summer 2010): 33-52.

————. Ukraine and the West." *Survival* 48, no. 1 (Spring 2006): 93-110.

Łapczynski,Marcin. "The European Union's Eastern Partnership: Chances and Perspectives." *Caucasian Review of International Affairs* 3, no. 2 (Spring 2009): 143-155.

Magen, Amichai. "The Shadow of Enlargement: Can the European Neighbourhood Policy Achieve Compliance?" *The Columbia Journal of European Law* 12, no. 2 (Spring 2006): 384-427.

Mendez, Carlos, Fiona Wishlade and Douglas Yuill. "Conditioning and Fine-tuning Europeanization: Negotiating Regional Policy Maps under the EU's Competition and Cohesion Policies." *Journal of Common Market Studies* 44, no. 3 (2006): 581-605.

Moravcsik, Andrew. "Preferences and Power in the European Community: A Liberal Intergovern-mentalist Approach." *Journal of Common Market Studies* 31, no.4 (December 1993): 473-524.

Moroney, Jennifer D. P. "Frontier Dynamics and Ukraine's Ties to the West." *Problems of Post-Communism* 48, no. 2 (March/April 2001): 15-24.

Müftüler-Baç, Meltem, and Yaprak Gürsoy. "Is There a Europeanization of Turkish Foreign Policy? An Addendum to the Literature on EU Candidates." *Turkish Studies* 11, no. 3 (September 2010): 405-427.

Olga Oliker. "Ukraine and the Caspian: An opportunity for the United States." *RAND Issue Paper* 198. Santa Monica, CA: RAND Corporation, 2000.

Olsen, Johan, P. "The Many Faces of Europeanization." *Journal of Common Market Studies* 40, no.5 (2002): 921-52.

Pelkmans, Jacques. "How Social is European Integration?" *Bruges European Economic Policy Briefings,* no. 18 (September 2007).

Petrov, Roman. "Legal Basis and Scope of the New EU-Ukraine Enhanced Agreement:Is There Any Room for Further Speculation?" *Max Weber Programme Working Papers*. San Domenico di Fiesole, Italy: European University Institute, 2008.

Samokhvalov, Vsevolod. "Relations in the Russia-Ukraine-EU Triangle: 'Zero-Sum Game.'" *Occasional Paper* No. 68. Paris: European Union Institute for Security Studies, 2007.

Schimmelfennig, Frank, and Hanno Scholtz. "EU Democracy Promotion in the European Neighbourhood: Political Conditionality, Economic Development and Transnational Exchange." *European Union Politics* 9, no. 2 (Spring 2008): 187-215.

Schimmelfennig, Frank, and Ulrich Sedelmeier, eds. "Governance by Conditionality: EU Rule Transfer to the Candidate Countries of Central and Eastern Europe." *Journal of European Public Policy* 11, no. 4 (August 2004).

Sedelmeier, Ulrich. "After Conditionality: Post-Accession Compliance with EU Law in East Central Europe," *Journal of European Public Policy* 15, no. 6 (September 2008).

―――. "Europeanisation in New Member and Candidate States." *Living Reviews in European Governance* 6, no. 1 (2011).

Simão,Licínia. "Discursive Differences and Policy Outcomes: EU-Russia Relations and Security in Europe." *Eastern Journal of European Studies* 2, no. 1 (June 2011): 81-95.

Solonenko, Iryna. "External Democracy Promotion in Ukraine: The Role of the European Union." *Democratization* 16, no. 4 (2009): 709-731.

Töller, Annette Elisabeth. "The Europeanization of Public Policies--Understanding Idiosyncratic Mechanisms and Contingent Results." *European Integration Online Papers* 8, no. 9 (2004).

Wijkman, Per Magnus. "Fostering Deep and Comprehensive Free Trade Agreements for the Eastern Partners." *Eastern Partnership Review* no. 8 (December 2011).

Wolczuk, Kataryna. "Adjectival Europeanisation? The Impact of EU Conditionality on Ukraine under the European Neighbourhood Policy." *European Research Working Paper Series*, Number 18 (August 2007).

———. "Implementation without Coordination: The Impact of EU Conditionality on Ukraine under the European Neighbourhood Policy." *Europe-Asia Studies* 61, no. 2 (2009): 187-211.

www.ingramcontent.com/pod-product-compliance
Lightning Source LLC
Chambersburg PA
CBHW081830280526
45789CB00007B/2408